Themes in Social Anthropology

Kinship, honour and solidarity

Themes in Social Anthropology
edited by David Turton and Marilyn Strathern

Buddhism in Life
The anthropological study of religion and the
Sinhalese practice of Buddhism
Martin Southwold

Sacrifice in Africa
A structuralist approach
Luc de Heusch

Initiation
Jean S. de la Fontaine

The appropriation of nature
Essays on human ecology and social relations
Tim Ingold

Ladislav Holy

Kinship, honour and solidarity

Cousin marriage in the Middle East

Manchester University Press
Manchester and New York
Distributed exclusively in the USA and Canada by St. Martin's Press

Copyright © Ladislav Holy 1989

Pulished by Manchester University Press
Oxford Road, Manchester M13 9PL, UK
and Room 400, 175 Fifth Avenue,
New York, NY 10010, USA

Distributed exclusively in the USA and Canada
by St. Martin's Press, Inc.,
175 Fifth Avenue, New York, NY 10010, USA

British Library cataloguing in publication data
Holy, Ladislav, *1933*–
   Kinship, honour and solidarity: cousin
marriage in the Middle East.—(Themes
in social anthropology).
1. Middle East. Marriage
I. Title   II. Series
306.8'1'0956

Library of Congress cataloging in publication data
Holy, Ladislav.
   Kinship, honour, and solidarity: cousin marriage in the Middle
East / Ladislav Holy.
     p.   cm.—(Themes in social anthropology)
   Bibliography: p.
   Includes index.
   ISBN 0-7190-2890-6
    1. Cross-cousin marriage—Middle East.   2. Marriage customs and
rites—Middle East.   3. Middle East—Social life and customs.
I. Title.   II. Series.
GN635.N42H65   1989
306—dc19   88-31479

ISBN 0 7190 2890 6   *hardback*

Phototypeset in Hong Kong
by Best-set Typesetter Limited

Printed in Great Britain
by Anchor Press Ltd, Tiptree, Essex

Contents

Acknowledgements	*page*	vii
Introduction: The problem of 'preferential patrilateral parallel cousin marriage'		1
1 The analytical and cultural meanings of the preference for FBD marriage		15
2 Pragmatic functions of FBD marriages and the marriage pattern		45
3 The right to the FBD and the expressive aspect of patrilateral parallel cousin marriage		72
4 Agnation, power and the symbolic significance of FBD marriage		93
5 Preference for FBD marriage in context		105
References		129
Index		139

To the memory of Emrys Peters

Acknowledgements

I wish to express my sincere thanks to the following friends and colleagues who were kind enough to read various drafts of this essay: Richard Fardon, Emanuel Marx, Kay Milton, David Riches, Marilyn Strathern, Richard Tapper and David Turton. Whilst they must not be held responsible in any way for the final product, their valuable comments helped me considerably to clarify and sharpen my argument and their incisive criticism often forced me to formulate better a number of points. I owe a debt of gratitude to them all. My thanks are also due to the two anonymous reviewers who made helpful comments on the version of the manuscript first submitted to the publishers, to Mrs Stella Peters who kindly allowed me to use Emrys Peters's photograph for the cover illustration, and to Paul Baxter who helped to select it. I am grateful finally to Helen Smith and Sybil Davis for their substantial typing assistance.

Introduction

The problem of 'preferential patrilateral parallel cousin marriage'

Until very recently, the discussion of specific problems of Middle Eastern ethnography has had only limited impact upon wider theoretical concerns of social anthropology. One noticeable exception to this has been the discussion of patrilateral parallel cousin marriage, i.e. the marriage of a man to the daughter of his father's brother, or to a kinswoman referred to by the same term as the genealogical father's brother's daughter (FBD). Stronger or weaker preference for this type of marriage is expressed in a number of societies and communities throughout the Middle East,[1] and in many of them the number of actual marriages between the children of two brothers or classificatory brothers is statistically significant in relation to other types of marital union. This phenomenon has attracted a great deal of the analytical attention of Middle Eastern specialists, for many of whom it has become the key problem of Middle Eastern ethnography. But FBD marriage is significant not only within this narrow regional context. It represents a striking exception to the principle of exogamy and, because it unites people who are already united and between whom there is, in a structural sense, no sociological difference, it plays precisely the opposite role from that played by marriage throughout most of the world. For these reasons it has also attracted a considerable amount of attention in the general anthropological discussion of kinship and marriage.

Given this amount of attention, an essay which has as its topic the 'problem of patrilateral parallel cousin marriage' should probably start with an apology for bringing up yet again this old 'anthropological favourite' (Geertz 1979: 370). But I do not think that any apology is needed. It is true that most anthropological accounts of marriage in the Middle East have focused to a large extent on the the causes, functions, meanings and structural consequences of this type of marriage. Many ethnographic studies paying special attention to it and a number of analyses of it are now available. But it is also true that this extensive literature does not always provide answers to all the questions which one may ask about it.

This essay tries to bring together the existing literature, which is quite disparate and highly variable in its attention to ethnographic detail and in the degree of its analytical sophistication, and in so doing tries to pinpoint its common underlying concerns as well as the points of disagreement. In this respect, it is meant to be both a summary of the 'state of play' and a critique. By highlighting the issues which seem to be germane to the understanding of marriage preferences in the Middle East, it aims to throw some light not only on the old 'problem of patrilateral parallel cousin marriage' but also on some of the wider issues which concern the understanding of Middle Eastern society and culture in general.

At many points in my discussion, I raise questions which cannot adequately be answered on the basis of our present ethnographic knowledge. Descriptions of the indigenous conceptualisations of kinship and affinity, of the local models of gender relations, or of the role of ideology in shaping the actors' economic and political strategies are just a few examples of accounts which are conspicuously missing in much of the existing ethnographic writing on the Middle East. The essay as a whole implies that we need to pay more systematic attention to people's own models and conceptualisations, if we are to advance our understanding of the constitutive relationship between their marriage preferences and other elements of the socio-cultural reality in which these preferences exist and from which they derive their functions and meanings.

FBD marriage and the problems of anthropological explanation

Although a great deal of analytical attention has been paid to marriages between children of two brothers in various Middle Eastern communities, patrilateral parallel cousin marriage still appears to be a disparate phenomenon. This is due to a whole range of factors, one of which is the unfortunate tendency to generalise from one, often highly specific, ethnographic case to the whole area of the Middle East. Depending on the perceived significance of this type of marriage in one specific ethnographic setting, it is then in a blanket fashion either ascribed or denied significance in the rest of the area in which it has been reported. The varying analytical tradition is another contributing factor. The explanations of FBD marriage range from those which see it as psychologically motivated, through those which see it as functional in attaining various practical goals, to those which see it as instrumental for the reproduction of the social structure of which it is itself a part. Ultimately, the image of

FBD marriage as a disparate phenomenon does not derive so much from the fact that the data are disparate, and that the social significance of this type of marriage is extremely varied, as from the fact that specific theoretical presuppositions have always guided decisions about what can be counted as relevant data and how the significance of these data should be construed.

In this essay, I discuss patrilateral parallel cousin marriage against the background of these often implicit theoretical presuppositions and, more generally, against the background of some of the problems of anthropological explanation. In this respect, the essay as a whole attempts to show how the handling of this type of marriage in anthropological debate has rested on a number of general assumptions about explanation. By making these assumptions explicit, it tries to explore the question of what can and cannot be explained through methods of anthropological enquiry, and in doing so it pays particular attention to the concepts of function, meaning and context. In spite of all the changing fashions or epistemological shifts in anthropology, these three concepts constitute the perennial linchpins of our interpretations. Of the three concepts, function and meaning have been the subjects of a considerable amount of scrutiny. Context, on the other hand, has always remained 'a wastebasket label, to explain away an array of fuzzy phenomena, too complicated to understand' (Keesing 1972: 28, n. 5). I argue, however, that defining properly the relevant context of the studied phenomenon is the first necessary condition for its adequate explanation. To my mind, neither the positivistic functional nor the semantic style of investigation in social anthropology has satisfactorily solved the problem of context definition. The reasons are not difficult to grasp. Both the function or purpose and the meaning of a phenomenon, like the purpose and meaning of a statement, are constructed through its interpretation. When trying to comprehend the function or meaning of a statement, act or object, we place it in various possible contexts in our effort to interpret it. The difficulties of specifying precisely what constitutes the relevant context, and of marking the context's boundary, arise from the fact that the specification of the context is itself the result of interpretation. In this sense, function and meaning are as much context-dependent as context is function- or meaning-dependent.

It seems to me that, in our effort to come to grips with the meaning of social and cultural phenomena, we have too hastily disregarded the dialectical relationship between meaning and context and tried to solve the problem of meaning by concentrating on only one aspect of this dialectical relationship: the effect of context on meaning. While meaning became problematic, context was, as it were, taken for granted. Phenomena were treated as if they were inherently part of a specific context and the problem was reduced to identifying it; we have too easily overlooked the fact that the context of the phenomenon does not exist out there for us to grasp but is itself, like the meaning, the result of our interpretation.

Patrilateral parallel cousin marriage seems to be particularly suitable for illustrating and elaborating some of these problems of explanation, since it is a phenomenon which has challenged, in many ways, the conventional anthropological wisdom. This phenomenon is difficult to reconcile with the accepted theoretical approaches to kinship and marriage (Fernea and Malarkey 1975: 188; Barnard and Good 1984: 166), and one of the favourite solutions to this problem has been to explain it away by reference to its often low frequencies (Anderson 1982: 7). Another favourite strategy has been to account for it 'in an *ad hoc* fashion more by translating native discourse into sociology than analysing it' (ibid).

Many other solutions to this 'problem' have been similar to those proposed by anthropologists to the 'problem' of Melanesian descent groups. They have either denied the significance of agnatic descent in Middle Eastern societies or suggested a discordance between the ideology of descent and the actually-observable pattern of social relations (Verdon 1981: 247). In many ways, such 'solutions' have only aggravated the problem and raised further questions. For example, if agnation is only a shadowy background against which real politics are played, what is the function of agnatic ideology and why do the actors delude themselves by subscribing to it so strongly? Confronted with these problems, some anthropologists have openly declared patrilateral parallel cousin marriage to be a phenomenon which cannot be explained sociologically, or one which occurs in settings so widely different economically, politically and culturally that, although it is possible to explain it within the specific context of one society or community, it is impossible to formulate generalisations about it which would be cross-culturally valid. It is a phenomenon which seems effectively to have eluded our explanatory efforts.

Quoting Cohen, that 'there can be no single sociological explanation for this kind of marriage' since it 'can be found in diverse social systems with diverse combinations of factors' (1965: 120, n. 1), Davis concludes his discussion of FBD marriage with the note that it is now 'clearly inappropriate' to look for its explanation (1977: 218). A similar view is offered by Bourdieu, who suggests that 'marriages which are identical as regards genealogy may ... have different, even opposite meanings and functions, depending on the strategies in which they are involved', and that 'any two marriages between parallel cousins may have nothing in common' (1977: 48). Similarly, Goody expresses doubt whether 'a general explanation' of marriage to the father's brother's daughter, 'either in a specific instance or overall, can be satisfactory' (1983: 43). It would thus seem that preferential patrilateral parallel cousin marriage is another of those analytic categories, without an intrinsic unity, which refer to a polythetic class of phenomena like marriage (Needham 1971: 5 ff.; Rivière 1971: 57 ff.) or witchcraft (Crick 1976: 112 ff.), an 'odd-job' phrase – 'very handy in all sorts of descriptive sentences, but worse than misleading in comparison and of no real use at all in analysis' (Needham 1971: 7–8).

The anthropologists' construct of preferential FBD marriage

Most classical objects of anthropological interest, like the 'segmentary lineage structure', the 'system of indirect exchange', etc., are anthropologists' constructs whose counterpart in the realities of the peoples who are supposed to have or to operate them in difficult to locate precisely. The reason is that, though they are our own abstractions formulated so that we can cope cross-culturally with the diversity of social processes and cultural forms, they have become reified through our analytical practice; for all practical purposes they are then threated as objects existing in the reality which we purportedly study. 'Patrilateral parallel cousin marriage' is one such construct.

Once we realise that many objects of our interest are our own constructs, we are led to an inevitable conclusion about the difficulties which we encounter when we try to cope analytically with them. Such difficulties do not reflect the culturally-specific or multifunctional nature of these objects which prevents us from formulating cross-culturally valid generalisations about them. Like the objects themselves, they are also of our own making. And if we have ourselves created the difficulties which ultimately defeat our explanatory efforts, we should be able to overcome them through deconstructing again the constructs which we have created in the first place. Instead of analysing again and again this society's or that society's reality in terms of our own constructs, in the faint hope that some light will eventually be thrown on it through this procedure, we had better start by analysing our own constructs.

Since the mid-1950s there have appeared a number of studies concerned with a phenomenon which became known as 'preferential patrilateral parallel cousin (or FBD) marriage' (Barth 1954: 164; Ayoub 1959: 266; Murphy and Kasdan 1967: 2). As a first step in defining this phenomenon precisely, it is apposite to ask what are its discriminating features, and how can one recognise a 'preferential patrilateral parallel cousin marriage' as such? This is a question to which the corpus of writing devoted to its analysis and explanation does not give a very good answer. There are usually three kinds of data which are taken as manifestations of preferential FBD marriage:

1 The actors' statements to the effect that such a marriage is a particularly good one or a better one than other marriages, or that it is particularly desirable.
2 The existence in the given culture of the rule which stipulates that a man has a right to marry his FBD and that no other man can marry her unless her FBS chooses not to exercise his right or expresses his consent to her marriage to another man.[2]
3 A pattern of contracted marriages such that the number of men who actually marry their patrilateral parallel cousin is significantly higher than it would be if their marriages were random, and which thus indicates that the asserted preference is actually enacted in behavioural practice.

But to what extent can these different kinds of data be seen as informing about one and the same thing? On closer inspection it appears that they relate to widely different aspects of social and cultural reality. The first two are informative about the actors' notions, i.e. about the ideals they entertain and about the norms to which they subscribe; the third is informative about the cumulative product of individual actions.

The construction of the object of study circumscribed as 'preferential patrilateral parallel cousin marriage' is a logical outcome of assuming that the various kinds of data imply one another. Thus, for example, the existence of the preference for marriage between patrilateral parallel cousins in a given culture is assumed to be isomorphic with and therefore deducible from the pattern of actually-contracted marriages. But to what extent is this assumption legitimate? This question is of practical significance for a great number of analyses of 'marriage preferences' in the Middle East. The notion that a preference for FBD marriage is only the most extreme expression of preference for 'endogamy at a almost every level of social organisation which the society recognises', which has informed a number of subsequent analyses, was originated by Ayoub (1959: 266) solely on the basis of her analysis of the observable marriage pattern, in the absence of any explicit statements by the actors to the effect that endogamous marriages are consciously preferred to others. On purely logical grounds, it would seem that the form of the marriage pattern alone cannot be taken as indicative of the existence of any specific preference, for the assumed preference which is taken as generating the observable marriage pattern operates on the pattern only at the statistical level and not necessarily at the causal level. The possibility cannot be excluded that 'more than a random number of such marriages are made because they are favoured for extraneous reasons' (Pitt-Rivers 1977: 163). The pattern can be generated by the actors choosing spouses on the basis of criteria or qualifications other than membership of a specific group or category. If more women within the group than outside it possess the desired qualifications, the pattern can then display more than a random number of intra-group or intra-category marriages. In short, the marriage pattern alone does not indicate whether there is a discrepancy between the reasons the actors actually followed in their marriage choices and the reasons the analyst thinks they followed. Should such a discrepancy exist, translating the actual reasons the actors followed into the reasons the analyst thinks they followed completely changes the meaning of the actors' actions. The postulated preference is then solely the result of the analytical procedure employed and not part of the social or cultural reality studied.

Similarly, in what sense can a man's right of prior access to his FBD be taken as a manifestation of preference for marriages between patrilateral parallel cousins? The existence of a culturally-recognised right to perform a certain action can hardly as such be taken as an indication of the culturally-recognised preference for such action. This would require us to assume something which our everyday experience clearly contradicts, namely that the actions which we have a right to perform are the actions which we actually prefer to perform. Does it then mean that a man's right to marry his FBD is a manifestation of the preference for marriage to an FBD, not as such but only in so far as it is constantly exercised? In that case the overt manifestation of the existence of the preference would again be the statistical occurrence of FBD marriages. The interpretation of such occurrence as a manifestation of a culturally-existing preference would again ultimately be based on an a priori assumption that it is this preference and not some unanalysed extraneous reason that generates the observable pattern. As long as the right of a man to marry his FBD can be linked to the culturally-expressed preference only through the actual marriage practice, the connection between the man's right to marry his FBD and the existing preference for such marriages is not unequivocally intrinsic, and one cannot be taken for the manifestation of the other.

When the various kinds of data on 'preferential patrilateral parallel cousin marriage' are treated by the analyst as informing about the same thing, nothing which meaningfully exists in the reality known to and lived by the actors is explained. What is being explained is only the anthropologist's construct, in which data on people's notions and data on their actions converge. In consequence, it is impossible to relate this explanation back to the socio-cultural reality of the peoples studied and to say whether what was being explained are the observable actions (i.e. why some or most patrilateral parallel cousins marry one another), the cumulative effect of such individual actions (i.e. the marriage pattern) or the proclaimed ideals and norms subscribed to (i.e. why the patrilateral parallel cousin marriage is considered ideal or why the right of a man to his FBD is recognised).

What is even worse is that it is assumed that the explanation of any one of the manifestations of 'preferential patrilateral parallel cousin marriage' automatically accounts for all its other manifestations. Thus one kind of reasoning (discussed in more detail in Chapter 2) assumes that the reasons for the observable actions (i.e. the reasons for patrilateral cousins marrying one another) are congruent with the reasons for FBD marriages being considered as binding or enforceable.

Another kind of reasoning assumes that the explanation of the preference for FBD marriage is congruent with the explanation of the observable marriage pattern, thus creating a distinct impression that the whole system of marriage in Middle Eastern societies can be adequately accounted for by explaining patrilateral parallel cousin marriage. The unfortunate outcome of this latter approach is that some writers have taken exception to it to such an extent that they have shunned the problem of parallel cousin marriage completely and concentrated on other aspects of the observable marriage pattern. For example, in his textbook on anthropology of the Middle East, Gulick does not even mention it as a problem that has occupied numerous analysts, and alludes to it only briefly in his discussion of marriage choices (1976: 220–1). Fernea and Malarkey openly declared it to be no longer a 'key problem' (1975: 189).

Preference for FBD marriage as a cultural notion

Although it may seem paradoxical, any progress in the explanation of the phenomenon which we have chosen to call 'preferential patrilateral parallel cousin marriage' can be achieved only when we realise that this anthropological construct has no unambiguous and specific referent in the social and cultural reality of various Middle Eastern societies. Their members entertain more or less clearly-formulated ideas that some marriages are good or desirable and others not so good or desirable; they sometimes recognise rules which given to certain individuals the right to claim certain others as their spouses; and they choose specific individuals as their spouses (or have them chosen for them by specific others). All these different manifestations of 'preferential patrilateral parallel cousin marriage' connote phenomena which exist in different senses and refer to different levels or domains of reality. In the simplest possible terms, one of these domains is formed by the notions or ideas people hold and communicate to one another, and the other by the actions they actually perform.[3] These two domains of reality are neither congruent with one another nor even imply one another. Their relationship is not logical but contingent and has to be treated as problematic (Holy and Stuchlik 1983).

This requires an analysis which does not confuse the explanation of the existing notions with that of the observable actions. Such analysis need not assume that the notions and the actions are completely independent; they are obviously related. In most existing analyses, this interrelation has already been presupposed. Thus Needham, for example, considers preference to be a rule 'governing the acquisition of a spouse' (Needham 1958: 75). On this view, marriages with persons in the preferred category automatically follow from the fact that such marriages are the cultural preference. In other words, the preference is seen as directly linked to actual marriages and the expressed preferences are treated as a cultural model for actual behaviour. But in my view it is not up to the analyst to arbitrate on the relationship between people's cultural notions (preferences) and their actions (marriages they actually contract), or to assume a priori what it is; it has to be treated as problematic. In other words, it is this relationship itself which has to become the object of the investigation.

Although the existing anthropological analyses have been, for the most part, explicitly concerned with the institution or custom of preferential patrilateral parallel cousin marriage, not all analysts have given equal weight to the various kinds of data which have been seen as its manifestation. Irrespective of their differing theoretical orientations (for the survey of theories guiding some older analyses see Khuri 1970; Hilal 1972; Fernea and Malarkey 1975: 188–91; Kressel 1986), some of them were concerned primarily with accounting for the expressed marriage preferences while others were primarily concerned with accounting for the observable actions and their resulting pattern. This essay is explicitly concerned with explanation of the expressed *preference*,[4] a phenomenon that clearly belongs to the notional, cognitive or cultural level of social reality. It pays only secondary attention to the observable actions, which exist at a different level of reality, and it pays attention to them only when they can be taken as unambiguous indications of existing preferences.

This has a direct bearing on something that has not been sufficiently appreciated in the discussion of the patrilateral parallel cousin marriage, namely that 'Why do cousins marry one another?' is a different and separate question from 'Why are cousins preferred as spouses?' The latter question is not answered by providing an answer to the former one. When the problem is to explain why cousins marry one another, the existence of the culturally-expressed preference is taken as given; what is to be investigated is why, to what extent, and under which specific circumstances it affects the actual marriage choices.

In his sensitive analysis of the selection of spouses among the Dhund of Pakistan, which treats the relationship between actors' notions and their observable actions as problematic, Donnan (1985) argues that marriages between kin cannot be explained simply in terms of the Dhund preferences for this type of marriage, in spite of the fact that the majority of spouses are mutually related (see also Bradburd 1984 for a similar argument). The actual spouses are chosen not simply because of the kinship relationship between them but for a number of pragmatic reasons, and the invocation of this relationship is a rhetorical device through which the respectability of the proposed match is construed and through which people support their case and bargain and negotiate with others. Each actual marriage choice is thus not a result of the preference for kinsmen, but the outcome of the interplay of a number of relevant factors. 'The preference for marriage with kinsmen is thus only one of several notions Dhund have about marriage and it becomes relevant to activity not by its mere existence, but only by people taking account of it' in the course of their 'strategy directed towards contracting the most advantageous marriage' (Donnan 1985: 195).

When it is to be explained why cousins are preferred as spouses, the problem which Donnan and Bradburd have addressed is redefined. What then becomes problematic about the preference is not why people follow or disregard it in their actual marriage choices but why it exists as a cultural notion.[5] This type of enquiry raises the important question of the relevant context in which the preference is to be seen.

Contexts of the preference

The almost exclusive emphasis on patrilateral parallel cousin marriage has been criticised for hampering the theoretical understanding of the Middle Eastern marriage system. This type of criticism points out two particular weaknesses of the prevalent analytical practice. Firstly, the explanation of the Middle Eastern marriage system in terms of 'the causes, meanings and structural implications of the practice of patrilateral parallel cousin marriage' leads 'to an almost complete neglect of other systematic patterns of marriage choice' (N. Tapper 1981: 387) and of other forms of marriage which almost always statistically predominate over marriages between cousins. Secondly, the understanding of the practice of FBD marriage is inhibited if this form of marriage is not seen in the context of other marriage choices which coexist with it. This criticism is good and valid if the problem to be explained is why people marry as they do. It does not apply, however, if the problem to be explained is why people subscribe to the view that marriages between cousins are the ideal, most desirable or best marriages. The notions and actions which have been collapsed under the unitary concept of 'preferential patrilateral parallel cousin marriage' have to be differently contextualised.

One obvious context in which the preference for FBD marriage has to be understood are all the other marriage preferences expressed in any given society or community. For the actors themselves, these preferences do not necessarily derive their meaning from the context of their marriage system but from quite different domains of their social and cultural reality. Since it tries to follow as faithfully as possible the actors' own contextualisation of their marriage preferences, this essay is not primarily concerned with the marriage system in the Middle East as such, but only with one of its features and with the wider contexts from which this feature derives its meaning. As numerous ethnographic accounts clearly indicate, there are many more aspects of marriage choices and strategies which have to be considered if the marriage system in the Middle East is to be grasped in its full complexity. Although this essay thus has a relatively narrow focus, I hope that it still makes some contribution to the understanding of some aspects of the Middle Eastern marriage system.

Of the three kinds of data mentioned earlier (p. 6), only the actors' verbal statements have a logically indisputable status as manifestations of the existence of culturally-recognised marriage preferences. They are, however, far from unambiguous as indications of what the preference expressed in any given society actually is (see Chapter 1).

When I specify the object of my interest as the preference for FBD marriages in the Middle East, it has to be understood that marriages to close kin beyond the very narrow range of prohibited degrees, including marriages to patrilateral parallel cousins, are *allowed* all over the Middle East. Although allowed and taking place everywhere in the area, in-marriages are probably not everywhere preferred to out-marriages in the sense of being seen as particularly desirable (Peters 1976: 61). The *preference* for FBD marriage is thus a more specific phenomenon than the *occurrence* of this kind of marriage; and while the former usually entails the latter, the reverse is not always the case. It also logically follows that the explanation of the preference for FBD marriage is not necessarily the same as the explanation of why this form of marriage is allowed or why it occurs; in other words, the question of why close in-marriages are premitted is a different question from why they are considered particularly desirable.

I am not attempting to address the first question, which raises the difficult problem of specifying the conditions under which no necessity was felt, at least in some specific cases, to establish alliances with strangers through the imposition of the rule of exogamy. It has been noted that the occurrence of marriages between close kin, sometimes as close as brother and sister (Hopkins 1980), was a characteristic feature of the marriage patterns of the ancient civilisations of the Mediterranean and the Middle East and of pre-Christian Europe (Luzbetak 1951; Tillion 1983; Goody 1983). All authors who have addressed the problem have attempted to link it to some characteristic aspects of the early civilisations of the Old World. Tillion connects the origin of the 'determination "not to exchange", to "keep all the girls in the family for the boys in the family"¹ (1983: 74) with the expansionist neolithic society of the Ancient World. According to her, the new economy, based on the cultivation of cereals, the domestication of animals and the emergence of cities, which developed in the Mediterranean Levant within the span of a few centuries, encouraged population explosion; this, in turn, released communities practising the new economy from the obligation to create alliances and they turned to in-marriages and away from out-marriages. Pitt-Rivers stresses the point that the exchange of women between groups reflects a consciousness of social equivalence and, like Tillion, he sees the growth of cities, accompanied by differentiation of class, and the conditions of political instability as circumstances favourable to the change towards a system of marriage strategy dominated by political values. When, under these circumstances, men's honour comes to be seen as vulnerable through the sexual behaviour of their women, sex acquires a special kind of political significance. From the moment the notion of honour is attached to female purity, women become the means of establishing dominance, for 'kinship loses its basis of reciprocity and becomes political and ego-centered, a competition in which the winners are those who keep their daughters and take the women of other groups in addition, giving only their patronage in exchange' (Pitt-Rivers 1977: 160 ff.). Goody, more broadly, stresses the positive association of FBD marriage in particular and in-marriage or endogamy in general with intensive agriculture and diverging devolution (1976).⁶

Whatever the particular thesis proffered, linking the occurrence of in-marriage with the rise of early civilisation may account for the fact that it exists among sedentary populations practising intensive agriculture based on the use of the plough and irrigation, among the city-dwellers and among the nomads, who 'live nonetheless in relation to the cities and under their political sway' (Pitt-Rivers 1977: 161). However, it leaves unexplained why in-marriage exists also among hoe agriculturalists and nomadic pastoralists whose economy, political organisation and system of inheritance and marriage prestations is certainly closer to that of the 'savages' (Tillion 1983) who forge alliances through exogamous marriages. To account for this we would have to assume that the preference for in-marriage spread to them through diffusion from the original centre of its emergence somewhere in the cradle of the ancient civilisation. Even if that could be shown to be so, we would still be left with the problem of explaining why they adopted as desirable a marriage practice that developed in response to the emergence of demographic conditions and economic and political relations quite different from theirs.

Unlike the authors mentioned above, I do not address the question of the *origin* of the marriage system that allows unions between close kin.

My sole concern is with suggesting an explanation for why such unions are deemed preferable by various populations which, in their economic, political and social circumstances, differ widely from one another as well as from the early civilisation of the Ancient World in which the kind of marriage for which they now express a preference is seen as having originated, but which are all located in the Middle East, an area which, in spite of its economic and political diversity, shares a common broad culture. In suggesting this explanation, I (like the actors themselves) consider the preference for FBD marriage in the context of the system of social action (Chapter 2) as well as in the context of the symbolic system of culture which endows the performed actions with their meaning (Chapters 3 and 4). The ultimate aim of the essay is to suggest an answer to the question why certain marriages in the Middle East are preferred to others. Such an answer, however, cannot be given unless the cultural meaning of the expressed preference is first understood. In consequence, such understanding represents not only an important but a necessary step in the overall explanatory strategy, for we cannot explain the reasons for the existence of a cultural phenomenon unless we have first properly understood its meaning. Appropriately, this is the the subject of the next chapter.

My interest in FBD marriage stems from my fieldwork among the Berti of Sudan,[7] who practise this kind of marriage and express a preference for it. Many of the problems discussed in this essay have been suggested directly by Berti ethnography, which for this reason figures prominently in the following pages. I also use other ethnographies, sometimes in considerable detail. Inevitably, these are only a few of the many potentially relevant bodies of ethnographic data, and their choice may seem arbitrary to the reader. My only justification for their selection is that they provided or suggested answers to the specific questions arising from my argument. I do not refer to numerous other ethnographies which also deal with FBD marriage or marriage systems in general but which do not provide answers to these questions. Obviously, I could not have read everything and I am sure that there are numerous books and articles which I should have referred to but which have escaped my attention. I hope, nevertheless, that even with these inevitable omissions, the points I am raising are adequately supported by the ethnographic accounts I refer to and I have to leave it to the reader to work out the application of my argument to other ethnographic contexts.

Notes to Introduction

1   Through the essay I use the term 'Middle East' very loosely to refer not only to the Middle East proper but also to the adjoining areas of Muslim North Africa

and Central Asia. In this loose usage, Middle East encompasses the area stretching from Morocco in the west to Pakistan in the east (Pierce 1971: 12) and includes Turkey and northern Sudan. My sole justification is that I do not try to define a culture area or to delineate its boundaries but merely to define the general terms of analysis for certain cultural notions which appear important within it.

2 Musil 1928: 137–8, 234; Granqvist 1931: 71–5; Dickson 1949: 116, 141; Barth 1953: 26; Patai 1955; Salim 1962: 48; Abou-Zeid 1965: 257; Bois 1966: 45; Cunnison 1966: 91; Bates 1973: 43, 61–3; 1974: 271; Geertz 1979: 373–4; Peters 1980: 139; Lancaster 1981: 59; Abu Zahra 1982: 73; Abu-Lughod 1986: 145, 286, n. 11.

3 The problem of the relationship between notions and actions is quite different from the dichotomy between 'ideal' and 'real' behaviour or from the difference between mechanical and statistical models (Lévi-Strauss 1969).

4 Though Lévi-Strauss (1969) contests the utility of a distinction between 'preference' and 'prescription', I found it useful for understanding the close kin marriages in the Middle Eastern context. I take a 'preference' to be an ideal sought by many but not all individuals of a given society and a 'prescription' to be a rule that is technically obligatory for all.

5 I prefer the neutral term 'notion' to the more usual 'rule', for the latter term already connotes a notion the purpose of which is to guide or regulate behaviour and thus already presupposes a specific relationship between a notion and observable actions. Such relationship, instead of being presupposed, should properly be the object of investigation. By *cultural* notion I mean a notion which is part of the actors' discourse and not of the anthropologists' analytical discourse. It is a notion of which the actors are aware, which they are usually able to formulate verbally and which they are certainly able to communicate to one another.

6 The origin of close kin marriage in Iran has also been traced back to Zoroastrianism, whose sacred texts have been interpreted by some scholars as enjoining marriages with sisters, mothers or daughters. Some scholars suggest that such marriages were actually practised, at least in the upper strata of Zoroastrian society (Tapper and Tapper 1988).

7 The Berti are sedentary cultivators living in the Northern Darfur Province of the Republic of the Sudan; they are Muslims and speak their own dialect of Arabic. Their social structure is outlined in Holy 1974.

Chapter 1

The analytical and cultural meanings of the preference for FBD marriage

One way out of the difficulties encountered in formulating cross-culturally valid generalisations about FBD marriage is to dissolve it as a meaningful category to be explained (see Bourdieu 1977: 48). However, it is one thing to dissolve an analytic category or concept for the sake of a better analysis, and quite another thing to dissolve people's own concepts and categories. That FBD marriage is recognised by the actors themselves as a meaningful category of marriage is abundantly attested by the widely prevailing notion that it is the ideal or best form of marriage or that it is at least a good or desirable marriage; in brief, it is attested by the preference for this type of marriage widely expressed by the actors themselves all over the Middle East and the adjoining areas of Muslim Africa and Asia. This preference is sometimes stretched so far that it is extolled as an ideal even if it rarely happens (Stirling 1965: 201; Pastner and Pastner 1972; R. Tapper 1979: 140–4; Lancaster 1981: 38, 61; Wikan 1982: 208). It will surely be accepted that it is impossible to express a preference for anything which in no meaningful sense exists, as those proposing the dissolution of the FBD marriage as a conceptual artifice would like us to believe.

If FBD is a culturally meaningful category for the actors, it is surely a methodological error to dissolve it for the sake of analytical convenience. Such an approach amounts to nothing more than a reformulation of the existing cultural notions in an effort to cope analytically with the studied reality. The reality is so much altered in the process that it becomes highly questionable to what extent the analysis can still be construed as an attempt to explain anything which has existed prior to it and which exists outside it. The assertion that FBD marriage cannot be sociologically explained effectively denies the significance of this type of marriage within the cultural and social reality of which it is a part, and amounts to an admission of analytical failure. Such failure is ultimately the result of an analytical practice which underrates the role of interpretation in the overall explanatory strategy. The way in which the preference for FBD marriage has been interpreted and meanings ascribed to it in existing anthropological analyses illuminates particularly well the various aspects of this basic problem.

The analytical meaning of the preference for FBD marriage

In a considerable number of anthropological writings on the subject since the time of Robertson Smith (1903: 72) and Wellhausen (1893: 437), the preference for patrilateral parallel cousin marriage has been interpreted as a preference for lineage endogamy. Patai presents such an interpretation quite emphatically. When concerned with 'Bedouin society as it actually operates', he is not distracted by the fact that 'the incidence of FaBrDa marriages constitutes, on average, probably 20 per cent of all marriages', for this society is 'an endogamous social system in which marriage brings together people who, in the great majority of cases, are *not* patrilateral parallel cousins' (Patai 1965: 334–5). The reason is that 'lineage or local endogamy, and not FaBrDa marriage, is the actual meaning of endogamy in the Middle Eastern context' (ibid.: 333–4). FBD marriage 'is always the most emphatic expression of patrilineal endogamy' (ibid.: 329).

This view, that descent-group endogamy is a characteristic feature of societies with preferential FBD marriages, has been criticised by Marx (1967: 222–3) and later attacked by Peters who, in his discussion of the marriage pattern of the Bedouin of Cyrenaica, points out that 'there is no question of this marriage pattern approaching an endogamous condition' (1980: 137). He rejects as a fiction the notion prevailing in much of the anthropological literature that Arabs, and by extension other Middle Eastern peoples, 'marry endogamously' on the grounds that their marriages are not endogamous either in the normative or in the behavioural sense: 'Marriage is permitted within the patrilineage, but there is no rule which prescribes it, and marriage outside is also permitted. Statistically the corporate lineage group is not an endogamous unit either' (ibid.).[1] He suggests two reasons for the analytical practice of treating FBD marriage as a problem of endogamy:

The only motive for viewing parallel cousin marriage as a problem of endogamy is the wish to simplify it by focusing the attention on men, and defining the marriage universe so widely and imprecisely that the majority of marriages are bound to be to parallel cousins of one sort or another, despite the fact that consanguinity between the spouses cannot be demonstrated; and by thoughtlessly casting aside the other relationships between spouses, sometimes when one of these is the nearest in terms of degrees (ibid.).

All this is true, but the criticism thus formulated may seem not to apply to the 'many offenders' Peters has in mind. Patai, whom I have singled out as an advocate of descent-group endogamy in Middle Eastern societies, makes it clear that these societies are not endogamous in the normative sense, i.e. in the sense that marriage within one's own patrilineage is prescribed, but merely in the sense that such marriage is given first preference (1965: 334). Preference for endogamy in Middle Eastern societies, in contradistinction to both normative endogamy and endogamy in the behavioural sense, is stressed by other analysts as well (e.g. Murphy and Kasdan 1959: 17, 22; 1967: 7; Ayoub 1959: 266; Pitt-Rivers 1977: 162). Peters's criticism may thus seem irrelevant, since these analysts obviously conceptualise endogamy differently from him. This criticism is, however, fully justified when it comes to the actual operationalisation of the concept of preferential endogamy in analytical practice. Patai does not state that endogamy but only that preference for it exists in the Middle Eastern society (1965: 325, 334). However, when he compares unilineal descent groups of the Middle Eastern society with the unilineal descent groups of sub-Saharan Africa, which are, of course, typically exogamous both in the normative and behavioural sense, he is forced by the requirements of typology and comparison to harden his concept of endogamy and to remove it from ethnographic reality (Murphy 1971: 59). In doing so, he equates it with normative obligation and treats it as a behavioural practice (Patai 1965: 334 ff., esp. 346). Similarly, Murphy and Kasdan (1959) and Barth (1973) analyse the structural features of societies with preferential FBD marriage in terms of a mechanical model in which such marriage is a predominant practice.

It might still be argued that characterising unilineal descent groups in Middle Eastern society as endogamous in the normative and the behavioural senses may be an exaggeration and an inexactitude following from the requirements of a specific analytical procedure, and that therefore the interpretation of the preference for FBD marriage as a preference for lineage endogamy remains unchallenged. In other words, as long as we understand endogamy in the limited sense of an asserted preference for marriage within the lineage, it is possible to see Middle Eastern society as endogamous.

But in fact two additional criticisms can be levelled against the interpretation of preference for FBD marriage as an instance of the more general preference for lineage endogamy. The first concerns the manner in which this interpretation is arrived at by inferring the preference from the observable marriage pattern.

The production of meaning

Following Wellhausen (1893: 437), Robertson Smith (1903: 72), Granqvist (1931: 78) and others, Ayoub (1959) rejected FBD marriage 'as being typologically distinct from any other form of endogamy' and redefined it 'by postulating it was not a class but simply one manifestation of a general preference towards endogamy' (Keyser 1974: 300, 301). As I have already mentioned, Ayoub reaches this conclusion on the basis of her statistical analysis of the observable marriage pattern. Now, such analysis can obviously indicate to what extent the culturally-expressed preference is followed in practice, but it cannot generate knowledge of what the preference is. This knowledge remains nothing other than the analyst's assumption. Unless the preference is conclusively identified independently, the statistical analysis merely shows that the analyst's assumption *may* by correct, not that it *is* correct. As far as the existence of the preference at the cultural level is concerned, it remains inconclusive. What is ultimately at issue is not a preference at all, but a tendency or observed incidence. As such, it presumably expresses the cultural notions held by the people; but without any actors' statements which indicate what their actions do express, there is no way of telling what those notions are. This is precisely the reason why Ayoub's analysis triggered off further testing of the possible significance of the frequency of FBD marriages through computer simulation and the employment of mathematical models (Gilbert and Hammel 1966; Goldberg 1967; Hammel and Goldberg 1971).

Though seemingly confirmed by subsequent tests, the view of the preference for FBD marriages as an expression of a more general preference for lineage endogamy has simply been axiomatically asserted. The reasons for this are simple: although the censuses subject to analysis are impressive and their statistical treatment often highly sophisticated, they remain inevitably circular. To perform a statistical analysis on any body of data, these data have somehow to be encoded, and the analyst's assumption about their meaning guides their coding for statistical treatment. As it is assumed a priori that what gives meaning to who married whom is the culturally-existing preference for descent-group endogamy, the data on who married whom are encoded in such a way as to reveal the degree to which this preference is actually followed in practice. If the practice conforms to the preference, its existence is seemingly confirmed. What is actually confirmed is not any culturally-existing preference but only the analyst's assumption about what gives meaning to his data. In this respect statistical analysis is not a substitute for the investigation of meaning. It is not a reflection of the meaning which the actors ascribe to their preferences but derives from the analyst's view of what are the significant structuring features of the socio-cultural system in question. This view was undoubtedly a logical outcome of the current anthropological epistemology.

An increased interest in Middle Eastern marriage in general and FBD marriage in particular has been noticeable since the mid-1950s. It was to a great extent a reaction to Lévi-Strauss's views, which became prominent in anthropology at this time and which considerably influenced the current conceptualisation of kinship, descent and marriage. The analytical meaning with which FBD marriage was endowed was the direct product of this reaction, in that it concentrated on the study of the type of marriage to which Lévi-Strauss did not pay any attention in his monumental work,[2] and in that it logically adapted tenets of his theory to the object of its own specific interest. In keeping with Lévi-Strauss's view that cross-cousin marriage is an expression of exogamy, parallel cousin marriage came to be seen as an expression of endogamy. Just as it became more or less generally recognised that the right marriage partner in the cross-cousin systems is not defined genealogically but in terms of belonging to a specific category, so the preferred spouse in the Middle East was not seen as genealogically defined (actual patrilateral parallel cousin) but as a member of a specific category (patrilineal descent group). This view has obviously been founded on, and is seemingly supported by, the widespread practice of applying the kinship terms for the genealogical patrilateral parallel cousin (or occasionally other close agnates) to all male members of the patrilineal group[3] (or occasionally the local community) (Uberoi 1971: 405; Maher 1974: 159). Robertson Smith understood the term *ibn 'amm* (father's brother's son) to mean 'literally a man of the same stock group' (1903: 72), and most later analysts followed his interpretation. They too glossed the term 'patrilateral parallel cousin', used by the actors in reference to the preferred spouse, as 'lineage member' and, in consequence, their analyses redefined marriage with a patrilateral parallel cousin as an intra-lineage marriage.

Many studies of Middle Eastern marriage patterns which employ intra-lineage and inter-lineage marriages as basic units of analysis, including those which explicitly deny the endogamous character of Middle Eastern society, are grounded in this assumption that FBD marriage is but one manifestation of a more inclusive category of intra-lineage marriages (these studies are too numerous to be cited here; Cohen 1965 and Antoun 1972 may serve as examples). If marriages with actual genealogical cousins are tabulated separately from other intra-lineage marriages, this is merely incidental and of no particular analytical significance.

This assumption can be sustained only if undue primacy is given to kinship terminological usage, and if the differentiation between first and other patrilateral cousins made at the level of actions and their concomitant norms is disregarded. Once that differentiation is taken into account, the validity of the assumption becomes doubtful. The Baggara of the Sudan and the Āl Murrah Bedouin of the Empty Quarter of south-eastern Arabia, whom I shall consider in detail later, make a clear distinction between first and more distant patrilateral cousins in reference to their marriage preferences (Cunnison 1966: 86, 91; Cole 1984:

179). In Kufr al-Ma village in Lebanon, the obligation that the girl be offered in marriage to her patrilateral cousin is more binding in the case of the first cousin than for the more genealogically distant cousins. Also the refusal to give a daughter in marriage to a brother's son is a more serious matter than the refusal to give her to a more distant agnate, and the pressure brought to bear on the offending party to comply with the expectation is much stronger in the former than in the latter case. In the Arab villages in Israel, where the right of a man to marry his patrilateral parallel cousin is recognised (Cohen 1965: 71, 72, 74–5, 121), the order of a particular cousin's priority right to marriage is determined by his genealogical nearness to the woman, in the sense that a first parallel cousin has priority over a second, etc. (ibid.: 121). Tillion echoes the same attitude for the Maghreb as a whole: 'the closer the relationship (between paternal cousins), the more satisfactory the marriage' (1983: 113). Patai (1955; 1962: chapter 2) gives further references to a similar differentiation between first and more distant agnatic cousins in older ethnographic writings. This differentiation is, incidentally, also expressed terminologically. While the term for the female patrilateral cousin (*bint 'amm*) applies to first as well as to more remote cousins, only a first patrilateral cousin in referred to as *bint 'amm luzum*, a literal translation of the suffix being 'must' or 'obligatory' (Antoun 1972: 48, 66–9, 74–7), or *bint 'amm waqif*, which literally means 'standing up' (Hilal 1972: 74). The Turkish speaking Yörük similarly distinguish 'true' (*öz*) from classificatory (*uşak*) cousins (Bates 1973: 65).

When marriage preferences are graded, or when a first genealogical patrilateral cousin is a more preferable spouse than a more distant cousin or a woman of the same lineage, it would probably be more accurate to talk of two different preferences rather than one: one for lineage endogamy and one for the patrilateral parallel cousin. Even if an FBD is preferred because she is a lineage member, this does not make the preference for the former simply a preference for the latter. On purely logical grounds, one preference cannot be explained as an expression of the other: if it were this, there would be no need to formulate it – one preference would be sufficient. The very fact that a preference for FBD is explicitly expressed as such by the actors means that it cannot be simply an expression of a preference for lineage endogamy.

Faced with the problematic fact that the FBD is singled out among all lineage members as the most preferred spouse, the proponents of the lineage endogamy theory suggest that it is the *most emphatic* or *most extreme* expression of endogamy. But such a view is again untenable, as it contradicts the very notion of lineage unity defined in terms of common descent which it simultaneously sees as motivating the preference. For A to be an extreme expression of B, B has to be something that comes in varying degrees or can be graded from mild to extreme. The notion of lineage endogamy is based on the recognition of a clearly-defined criterion which determines whether one is or is not a member of the lineage. Only if lineage membership could be graded, so that some people were lineage members to a greater degree than others, could an extreme expression of lineage endogamy possibly exist in any meaningful sense. As a lineage is often a corporate group, whose members are formally equals, this is unlikely to be the case.

Preference for FBD and other marriage preferences

The second criticism which can be levelled at the interpretation of the preference for FBD marriages as an expression of lineage endogamy concerns the fact that it has difficulty accounting for marriages with cousins other than patrilateral parallel ones.

Marriages with cross-cousins, matrilateral parallel cousins and other kin occur widely all over the Middle East, although it is often difficult to estimate their frequency because of the way in which the data on the relationship between the spouses have been encoded in existing analyses and thus already endowed with specific meaning prior to their statistical treatment. There is some evidence, for example, that marriages with MBD and MZD occur in Ayoub's Druze village. A man's marriage with either of these relatives is categorised by Ayoub as an intra-family marriage if the woman is 'independently a member of his kin group' (1959: 267), and apparently as an inter-village marriage if she is not. Given this categorisation, it is difficult to establish what is the frequency of such marriages with matrilateral cousins and quite impossible to ascertain what may be their meaning.

The occurrence of marriages with cross-cousins, matrilateral parallel cousins and other kin can be reconciled with the lineage endogamy theory only when it is assumed that marriages with cousins other than patrilateral parallel ones are not preferred any more than marriages among strangers. This assumption underlies, for example, Rosenfeld's analysis of the marriage pattern of Moslems and Christians in an Arab village in Isreal. He categorises marriages as parallel cousin marriages, clan marriages (which include classificatory parallel cousin marriages), intra-village marriages and inter-village or stranger marriages. According to him they are preferred in this order (1957: 35, 42), and his statistical analysis clearly indicates that such preference is to a remarkable extent enacted in behavioural practice.

Marriages with MBD and MZD occur in Rosenfeld's village, and in his analysis they are included in the category of inter-village or stranger marriages (ibid.). Assuming that his transcription of kinship relations between spouses is not based on his own reading of their connection from elicited genealogies but follows the actors' own classification, it is doubtful that the actors themselves would categorise MBD or MZD as 'strangers'. More importantly, there is some evidence that at least FBD–FBS and FZD–MBS marriages are conceptualised in the same way by the villagers themselves: Rosenfeld mentions that a compensation must be paid to the paternal and maternal uncles if the girl is not married to their son or to a member of their lineage (ibid.: 47). This makes it rather doubtful that these two types of marriages are at the same time differently categorised as to their desirability.

Preference for marriages with cousins other than patrilateral parallel ones seems to occur widely in various areas of the Middle East: it is, in fact, often reported as being explicitly stated by the actors themselves next to the preference for patrilateral parallel cousins.[4] The significance of marriages with these other cousins becomes even more apparent when we take into account censuses of contracted marriages in which the recorded cases are encoded in terms of genealogical relations between the spouses rather than in terms of their membership of specific categories. Such censuses clearly indicate that marriages with cousins other than patrilateral parallel ones, as well as other relatives, not only occur widely in he Middle East alongside marriages between patrilateral parallel cousins but quite often outnumber them.[5] Their occurrence is higher than it would be if marriages beyond the narrow range of prohibited degrees were fully independent of kinship considerations, and clearly indicates that the expressed preference for other cousins is in operation alongside the preference for FBD–FBS marriages.

Given this fact, the lineage endogamy theory cannot hold unless it is assumed that marriages with other cousins are preferred only because they are actually marriages within the lineage. It is the membership of the spouses in the same lineage which is, for the actors, the significant criterion, and not the actual genealogical connection between them, however close in terms of degrees it may be. This assumption underlies Murphy and Kasdan's analysis of patrilateral parallel cousin marriage. They argue that even reported marriages with MZD or MBD are endogamous as far as patrilateral parallel cousin marriage is the dominant preference, for MBD will be at the same time an FFBSD, that is a second-degree patrilateral parallel cousin. They venture to hypothesise that the Bedouin would interpret the relation in the latter way (1959: 22–3; cf. also Murphy and Kasdan 1967: 5). Their hypothesis of the patrilateral parallel cousin marriage as 'preferential endogamy within the agnatic line' (1959: 22) is thus based on the assumption of the overriding importance of agnation, the manifestation of this importance being the practice of tracing genealogical relationships in an agnatic line whenever possible.

Marriage preferences and cultural conceptualisations of kinship 23

Whatever the particular assumption entertained, the theory of the preference for FBD marriages as an expression of lineage endogamy is clearly predicated on the existence of a specific classification of marriages according to their desirability. It is a classification in which marriages with cousins other than patrilateral parallel ones are categorised by the actors alongside marriages with strangers and jointly opposed to the preferred marriages between direct and classificatory patrilateral parallel cousins: direct and classificatory patrilateral parallel cousins are to other cousins as preferred marriages are to ordinary marriages.

Marriage preferences and cultural conceptualisations of kinship

The existence of this system of classification, on which the theory hinges, can of course, be tested, and it is appropriate at this point to turn to at least a brief consideration of concrete ethnographic cases. Here, my scope is limited, for although there has been much analysis of the reasons for the existence of preferential FBD marriage, and of its structural consequences, the anthropological literature on the Middle East is distinguished not only by its lack of concern with the natives' mode of expression of their marriage preferences[6] and their own classification of contracted marriages, but also by its almost total neglect of the people's own conceptualisations of kinship. Since it is these issues that are germane to my present argument, I have been of necessity confined to ethnographic descriptions which provide at least partial answers to these questions, and to the data yielded during my own fieldwork among the Berti.

Berti

The only marriage prohibitions which the Berti recognise are those stipulated by the Koran. According to their understanding of the Koranic prescription, a man must not marry his own mother, mother-in-law, lineal grandmothers (FM, MM), lineal granddaughters (SD, DD), direct and half sisters, his own daughters and daughters of his brothers and sisters (BD, ZD), his direct paternal and maternal aunts (FZ, MZ), or any woman who has been nursed by the same woman as he has. The Berti do not extend their prohibitions on marriage to collaterals designated by the same kinship term as the prohibited women. Marriage with any kinswoman beyond the prohibited range is allowed. It is not kinship terminology which defines the category of prohibited women. This category is clearly defined by genealogical distance, and a woman designated by a specific kinship term (e.g. *ukht* – sister, or *binei* – daughter) can be either non-marriageable or a potential spouse, depending on her actual genealogical relationship to ego. A Berti can thus marry either a kinswoman or a stranger, i.e. a woman with whom he cannot trace any genealogical connection, and it is these two categories of marriageable women which the Berti compare and contrast when they discuss their marriage preferences in general terms.

Marriage among kin is a cultural preference for the Berti. People should, as they say, marry 'within the house' (*fi batun al bēt*) and not 'from outside' (*min barra*). Women are the wards of their kinsmen, whose right it is to marry them; only after the marriage needs of the kinsmen have been satisfied should the wards be given in marriage to strangers. Various common sayings clearly express this attitude: 'If we have not satisfied our hunger from our porridge, we do not give to other people' or, more briefly, 'it is from my porridge that I satisfy my hunger'; 'if you have water bags in your house, why should you go and borrow somebody else's?'; 'we have put our flour into our milk'.[7]

The Berti recognise all those to whom they can trace genealogical connection as their kinsmen (*ahal*); it is this category of people to whom the expression *fi batun al bēt* (as opposed to *min barra*) refers. Obviously, not all kinsmen are considered equally close. Kinship distance is evaluated in terms of genealogical distance from ego; but of two genealogically equidistant kin, the one who is paternally related is closer than the one who is related maternally. The Berti say '*amm agrab min al khāl, ubahāt agrab min akhwāl* ('the father's brother is closer than the mother's brother and paternal kin are closer than maternal kin'). The notion of the closer kinship of paternal than maternal relatives derives from the idea that bones are a more important part of the person's substance than flesh, as the latter cannot exist without the former but the former can without the latter, and ultimately from the conceptualisation of the reproductive process according to which it is the father's sperm from which the child's bones and sinews grow within the mother's womb while its flesh grows later from the mother's blood. Also consistent with this view of the reproductive process is the notion that kinsmen, both paternal and maternal ones, are closer than genealogically equidistant kinswomen and any connection traced through a man is closer than one traced through a woman. Expressed in terms of the relative value ascribed to agnation and cognation, it means that of two genealogically equidistant links the agnatic one is considered closer than the cognatic one; a genealogically closer cognatic link is, however, always closer than a more (even a slightly more) distant agnatic link. Cognation is the basic measure of kinship distance, with agnation used as a secondary criterion.

A certain number of marriages between kin are inter-generational. Most of them, however, are intra-generational, i.e. between cousins or classificatory cousins. It is intra-generational marriages, and particularly marriages between first cousins, which the Berti clearly have in mind when they compare and contrast marriages between kinsmen with those between strangers.

Although all first cousins are genealogically equidistant, they are not considered equally close by the Berti and they are graded in the following way in terms of their kinship distance from ego: FBS, FBD, FZS, FZD, MBS, MBD, MZS, MZD. These differences in kinship distance are, however, not reflected in the expression of preference for marriages with specific cousins. When the Berti compare marriages to kin with those to strangers, they insist that marriage with any cousin is a good one and that no cousin is potentially a better spouse than any other. This is a view expressed by both men and women and it derives primarily from consideration of the advantages of particular marriages in their economic context.

Another system of classification of marriageable women is based on contrasting patrilateral parallel cousins with all other potential spouses. According to this system, a marriage between patrilateral parallel cousins is preferable to any other marriage, including that with a more distant kinsman or kinswoman. This is a view expressed by men and it derives primarily from consideration of the advantages of particular marriages in their political context as well as from consideration of the relative ease or difficulty with which a particular marriage can be negotiated and arranged.

Classifying particular marriages as ones between patrilateral parallel cousins in descriptive analysis (even if this classification follows the native usage) requires a certain justification in the light of Peter's criticism of the descriptive and analytical primacy given to marriage with the FBD in the literature on the Middle East. He points out that the majority of first patrilateral cousin marriages contain a plurality of connections because the spouses have already been related not only as first cousins but in numerous other ways before their marriage: 'Thus, for example, a favoured marriage is a first parallel cousin marriage between the son and daughter of two full brothers who had themselves married first parallel cousins ... Almost invariably, these three kinds of marriages are described as first patrilineal parallel cousin marriages, as if this is the only relationship'. If fact, seven different modes of relationship exist between the spouses in this case (Peters 1980: 133–4) and there can be more of them in other cases, particularly in marriages between second or classificatory patrilateral parallel cousins (cf. Randolph and Coult 1968: 83, 87, 91; Lancaster 1981: 40).

Whether it is justified, in such cases, to treat the relationship between spouses as that of first cousinship, or whether all the plural connections (or some of them) have to be taken into account in analysis, is, however, not a conceptual but an empirical question. How the relationship between spouses should be classified for analytical purposes depends ultimately on how the people in question themselves classify it. The Berti invariably classify the relationship between a son and a daughter of two full brothers who have themselves married first parallel cousins as an FBD–FBS relationship and not an MZD–MZS relationship. For the man, his potential wife is *ukht, bit 'amm* (sister, the daughter of the father's brother); and for the woman, her potential husband is *akhu, wad 'amm* (brother, the son of the father's brother).

When multiple relationships exist between two people, the closest genealogical relationship takes precedence over more distant ones; and when two equidistant genealogical relationships can be traced between the people in question, the relationship traced through a person closer in kinship takes precedence over the relationship traced through a person less close in kinship. If a woman is simultaneously an FBD and an MZD, she will invariably be classified as an FBD because the father is more closely related than the mother. This classificatory principle is consistently applied in all cases. Thus, for example, the relationship between two people who are simultaneously FFBSD–FFBSS and MBD–FZS is classified as MBD–FZS relationship even by men;[8] for the Berti, unlike the Marri Baluch (Pehrson 1966: 42), the Awlad 'Ali Bedouin of Egypt (Abu-Lughod 1986: 56) and the Kabyles (Bourdieu 1977: 42), the agnatic relationship between these two individuals does not take precedence over their closer cognatic relationship.

When the Berti express their marriage preferences in general terms, they not only stress that people should marry 'within the house' and not 'from outside', but also that they should marry 'close' (*garīb*). A marriage between patrilateral parallel cousins is a marriage between the closest possible kinsmen beyond the prohibited range and this in itself makes it a normatively expected one. This does not mean, however, that marriages between classificatory patrilateral parallel cousins are preferred to marriages with first cross-cousins or first matrilateral parallel cousins. Also, when the Berti say, stating their marriage preferences in general terms, that a marriages with a woman from the same lineage (a category of marriages which includes those with classificatory patrilateral parallel cousins) follows in precedence a marriage with a first genealogical cousin and rates above a marriage with a stranger, they are not in any sense expressing preference for lineage endogamy. Equally, when they single out the patrilateral cousin marriage as an ideal one, this cannot be taken for an indication that this kind of marriage is for them a pure or ideal form of a wider principle of lineage endogamy.

Even when preference for marriage within the lineage is meaningful within the scale of preferences headed by a patrilateral parallel cousin, it is not in terms of lineage endogamy that these preferences are expressed but solely in terms of kinship distance. Marriage to a cousin is preferable to marriage within the lineage when close genealogical connections between spouses cannot be traced, not because the former kind of marriage is endogamous within a closer agnatic group that the latter but simply because the kinship relationship between spouses is closer. In the same way, marriage within the lineage is preferable to marriage outside the lineage because in the latter case no kinship relationship between the spouses is presumed to exist; although no exact genealogical connection may be traced between spouses if they are merely of the same lineage, it is, nevertheless, presumed to exist: the maximal lineage is the widest category of people to whom the term *ahal* may be applied.

Marri Baluch

Among the Marri, the range of women with whom marriage is proscribed is very narrow and includes only M, SW, FZ, MZ, Z and D (Pehrson 1966: 39; figures in parentheses in this section are page references to Pehrson). There is a distinct preference for marriages with particular women beyond the prohibited range which the Marri express in a similar way to the Berti by formulating it as a preference for marriages between kin (*wati*) (34; cf. also 57).

The term *wati* derives its meaning from its opposition to *seyyal* – 'stranger' (45) or 'unrelated social equal' (34). Other terms similarly opposed to *seyyal* are *jind* (literally 'one's own') and *aziz* (34–5). *Aziz* seems to have almost the same meaning as *wati*, but *wati* appears generally to be the widest term used to denote kin (35) and obviously denotes bilateral kin. Non-agnatic second cousins are regarded by the Marri as very distant relatives indeed, but the fact that they would on occasion be described as *waldein* (distant) *trizakht* (FZchild, MZchild, MBchild) indicates that they are still conceptualised as kinsmen, albeit distant ones. On he whole, like other categorical terms which the Marri use, *wati* lacks a clear criterion of genealogical distance by which its boundaries could invariably be defined (35). Its limits vary contextually according to situationally-determined extensions and denials of kin loyalties and demands (50). Members of the mother's lineage are often referred to as *seyyal*, especially by men; but exclusively matrilaterally-related persons, if they are close, may be categorised as *aziz* by women (35, 37, 45). In some contexts, distant patrilateral relatives are referred to as *seyyal* even by men (35), and some informants classified even agnatic cousins as *seyyal* in some situations (50).

There is no evidence in Pehrson's published texts that the Marri express their marriage preferences in terms of preference for marriages within a lineage (*waris*), a unit which always includes agnatic first cousins (40). Yet marriages between first patrilateral parallel cousins (*nakozakht*) represent 30 per cent of all marriages (57). Thirty-three per cent of marriages in tent camps and 21 per cent of marriages in Badra village were with agnates other than patrilateral parallel cousins, while 9 per cent of marriages in tent camps and 12 per cent of marriages in Badra village were with other, presumably non-agnatic, kin. Most of these letter marriages are probably classified as ones between *seyyal* by men, although not necessarily by women, who place more importance on female relatives and female links than men and whose conception of kinship comes 'nearer to embracing a bilateral kindred' than that of men (44–5).

In the marked absence of expressed preferences for marriages within a lineage, the observed preponderance of FBD–FBS marriages can be understood when it is seen as an outcome not only of the preference for marriages with kin but, as among the Berti, of the preference for the closest kin beyond the forbidden degrees.

Although the boundaries of the kinship universe contextually vary for the Marri from situation to situation, they have, again like the Berti, a clear notion of the relative proximity and distance of kinship (cf. 42) which they express by contrasting terms: *hakein* (duty), *sākein* (strong), *pelin* (line), *khāse* (proper) vs. *waldein* (distant), *dir-e* (far). Their kinship universe is structured by rating genealogical connections through men above those through women. Agnates are thus closer kinsmen than cognates, and indeed for many purposes only agnatic relationship is treated as proper kinship. The relationship between matrilateral parallel cousins is considered unimportant (35). In important contexts, children seem to regard even their own mother as a kind of affine (33, 34), although in other contexts this is modified by a fundamentally bilateral view of kinship.

The closeness of agnatic kinsmen is expressed in an 'axiom of Marri kinship': 'My share is on my father's side, on my mother's side there is nothing' (38). It is clearly reflected in the existing differences in genealogical knowledge, in the kinship terminological usage and in the extension of the incest ban. Whereas all men know their patrilineal ancestors and most of them know the name of their FFFF, the knowledge of even the closest maternal connections is vague and few people know the name of their MF (34). In reference terms, agnatic connection, even the more distant in the number of genealogical links, takes consistent preference over cognatic connection. Thus if parents are patrilateral parallel cousins, MF will be referred to as FFB (35). A man whose sister is married to his and her FBS may address her son as his ZS but refers to him as his FBSS.

A boy whose parents were FBSD–FFBS addressed his MB as such but was made by his father to refer to him by the proper agnatic term, as his FFBSS (42). Relations with wives of close agnates (F, FB, B, S and BS) are regarded as incestuous, whereas no extension of the incest ban takes place through women. Unlike sexual relations between BW and HB, those between WZ and ZH are not incestuous and occasionally do occur (89–90); equally, intercourse with MBW, unlike that with FBW, is not incestuous (39). As suspicions of adultery cannot be directed towards close agnates, a special relationship of trust exists between them: 'The Marri concept of *wati* ("close relative") seems to be primarily an expression of this kind of intimate trust and unity ...' (91).

Within the category of agnates, the degree of closeness is graded in terms of lineal and collateral distance, although this grading is different for the purpose of defining rights to property and to legal guardianship over women on the one hand and for the purpose of defining the degree of jural responsibility on the other hand (41, 63).

The Marri kinship universe is not only structured by consistent grading of agnates over cognates. Its other structuring feature is 'the dichotomization of male and female and the associated, very marked differentiation of the kinds of relationships that one can have to them respectively' (44). The important structuring principle is a distinction 'between agnates who perpetuate the agnatic relationship, that is, males, contrasted to other relatives' (39). There is a clear predominance given to the male line in kinship which leads to conceptualising father's sister and own sister as less than proper agnates; 'they are rather peripheral and non-essential relatives in the same way as matrilateral relatives' (44). All these relatives are assimilated into one category called *niagh* (38).

In the Marri way of grading kinship distance, the near male agnates are the closest relatives and the female members of the mother's lineage stand at the very edge of the recognised kinship universe. As one informant expressed it: 'The women of my mother's brother's lineage (*Mamakhel*) are nothing to me ...' (44).

Baggara

The ideal marriage for the Baggara is that between first patrilateral parallel cousins, followed in order of preference by that between cross-cousins provided that they are at the same time related as close agnates, that is, as the Baggara themselves express it, members of the same *surra*, a group of agnates of five or six generations' depth. Next in order of preference is marriage within *surra*, i.e. marriage between classificatory patrilateral parallel cousins. No special preference is given to marriages between matrilineal parallel cousins (Cunnison 1966: 9, 90, 91).

The Baggara thus classify marriages according to their desirability in the same way as the Marri Baluch do, by opposing marriages between agnates to those between cognates and strangers.

There is no information available on their notions about the relative value of agnation and cognation or on their way of evaluating kinship proximity and distance.

Although their terminological classification of cousins differs from that of the Marri Baluch, in that the existing agnatic relationship does not override the closeness of the cognatic link as far as the kinship terminological usage is concerned (Cunnison: personal communication), the Baggara nevertheless formulate their marriage preferences in a way which clearly points to be the overriding importance of agnation. Their classification of marriages according to their desirability would indicate that, as among the Marri Baluch, agnation is the basic measure of kinship distance, with cognation used as a secondary criterion: of two genealogically equidistant links, the agnatic one is considered closer than the cognatic one, while at the same time a genealogically more distant agnatic link is considered more important, as far as degree of kinship is concerned, than a genealogically closer cognatic link. This scale of evaluation has to define the limits beyond which agnatic connections would be too distant to override in importance close cognatic links. The limits of *surra* provide such a conceptual boundary.

In formulating their marriage preferences, the Baggara, like the Berti and the Marri Baluch, stress the closeness of a relationship rather than merely the membership of a specific group: 'they state that the closer the cousin, the better the marriage' (Cunnison 1966: 86). They do not merely prefer marriages within the *surra* to inter-*surra* marriages, but evaluate the desirability of intra-*surra* marriages according to the degree of the partners' closeness (ibid.: 91).

Āl Murrah

For the Āl Murrah, marriage preference is for the first patrilateral parallel cousin, followed by a classificatory patrilateral parallel cousin; the closer the classificatory cousin, the more desirable is the marriage. Next in order of preference is marriage to a real or classificatory cross-cousin who is not agnatically related, followed by marriage to a woman of full tribal status from within the Āl Murrah or any other Sharif Bedouin tribe. Men of shaikhly status follow political considerations in their marriage choices and, apart from marrying close agnates or cognates, also marry women from other shaikhly families of the Āl Murrah or of other tribes (Cole 1984: 179; see also Cole 1975: 71, 73).

The Āl Murrah thus also classify marriages according to their desirability by opposing marriages between agnates to those between cognates and strangers, and their marriage preferences also clearly point to the overriding importance of agnation.[9]

The cultural meaning of marriage preferences

Comparison of the four cases indicates specific differences as well as similarities in the cultural notions of the four peoples. In all four societies, marriage between patrilateral parallel cousins is a preferred or ideal form of marriage. However, in none of them is it the only preference. When all expressed preferences are considered, clear differences emerge in the system of classification of possible marriages according to their desirability. The Berti classification differentiates marriages between both close agnates and cognates, including marriages with FBD, as preferential ones and opposes them to marriages between distant agnates and strangers. In the Baggara, the Āl Murrah and most likely also the Marri Baluch systems of classification, it is marriages between close and distant agnates, including again marriages with FBD, which are preferred and opposed to marriages between cognates and strangers. The preference for FBD marriages has its meaning only within these systems of classification.

Since in different cultures marriages are differently classified as to their desirability, consideration of the existing systems of classification alone would seem to lead inevitably to the conclusion that preferential FBD marriage is a conceptual artifice without intrinsic unity. Given the context of the classification from which it derives its meaning, it may be construed as having different meanings in different cultures. Since the interpretation of the preference for FBD marriages as an expression of lineage endogamy is clearly predicated on the assumption of classification which opposes marriages between close and distant agnates to those between cognates and strangers, the dissolution of the preference for FBD marriages as a meaningful entity seems to be the inevitable logical consequence of the acceptance of such an interpretation. Where no lineage organisation exists the expressed preference for FBD marriages has a different meaning from where it does, and hence constitutes a phenomenon which has to be analytically distinguished from preference for FBD marriages in societies with lineage systems. In fact, this view has been clearly implied in some analyses of preferential FBD marriage.

Barth, who treats preference for patrilateral parallel cousin marriage as an instance of lineage endogamy (1954; 1973: 11), predicts that a high frequency of FBD marriages will be associated with a developed lineage organisation in which the lineage and its segments play an important role in armed conflict, and that it will be appreciably lower in villages with a different type of organisation. He supports his hypothesis with figures from the Kurdish Hamawand territory, where the frequency of marriages with actual, non-classificatory patrilateral parallel cousins amounts to 42.6% (1954: 167),[10] and from the feudally-organised southern Kurdish territory, where it drops to 13% (ibid.: 169; see also Barth 1953: 68), approximating the frequency reported from other areas of the Middle East (for rates of FBD marriages in different societies of the Middle East see Hilal 1972: 74). The difference in these figures is, no doubt, statistically significant and seems to lend clear support to Barth's argument. But the fact still remains that FBD marriage is a cultural preference even among the southern Kurds. And if the meaning of this preference in Hamawand derives from the context of political relations, its meaning among the southern Kurds must be different since this context does not apply.

Goldberg's analysis of marriage preferences among the Tripolitanian Jews in Israel shows that 'one of the kinship-oriented rules is "marry a close relative", including both patrilateral and matrilateral relatives' (1967: 189). In his conclusion he admits, nevertheless, to the view which is implied in Barth's analysis by suggesting that 'in other Middle Eastern communities *where lineage organisation is unimportant*, FBD marriage may sometimes best be seen as one type of marriage to a close kinsman' (ibid., emphasis added).

As I have said, it is one thing to dissolve the analyst's concept for the sake of a better analysis, and quite another thing to dissolve people's own concepts and categories. The preference for FBD marriages is not only clearly the people's own notion, but it exists in an area which, in spite of its apparent diversity, shares many features of a common culture. As it is expressed in virtually the same terms all over this area, it seems more justifiable to treat it as a part of that culture, and to interpret it analytically in a way which does not distort its cultural meaning, rather than to dissolve it as a conceptual artifice.

When it comes to this meaning, the notions which underlie the differences in the systems of classification become significant. They are remarkably similar in all the four societies in that the marriage preferences, of which the preference for FBD is just one, are formulated in terms of preferences for close kinsmen as opposed to distant kinsmen and strangers. The existing marriage preferences were explicitly formulated in these terms by the Berti and Marri Baluch, and the same preferences are strongly suggested by the Baggara and Āl Murrah ethnography.

The Rwala state a quite explicit preference for marriage with the closest possible kin by admitting that the ideal marriage would be between brother and sister, for 'only then could one be certain of their reputations and of having an identity of interests'. But brother–sister marriages would, of course, be incestuous, and this is also the reason why marriages between first patrilateral parallel cousins, although proclaimed as the ideal, are in fact disliked and most of the close in-marriages occur between classificatory cousins. The Rwala explain this by saying that first cousins are 'too like brother and sister' (Lancaster 1981: 60–1; see also Anderson 1982: 14).

Everywhere in the Maghreb, as Tillion points out, the paternal parallel cousin is referred to as *bint 'amm* – the daughter of the paternal uncle; but 'in songs, in the language of love, and even in daily usage, female cousins are usually spoken of as "my sisters", "my sister"'. The ideal marriage thus 'takes place with the female relative who, while not a sister, most resembles one'. The 'quest for a union with the nearest female relative' results in living 'in close proximity with people to whom one is bound by ties of consanguinity and even legal kinship (for uterine relations are, in many places, barely tolerated)' (Tillion 1983: 73–4).

The classification of marriages as to their desirability can usefully be seen as an articulation of this general preference for marriage between the closest kin. The differences of classification reflect the logical possibilities in computing closeness of kinship by ascribing different values to agnation and cognation. The preference for FBD marriages derives from the fact that, whatever value the actors ascribe to agnation or cognation, patrilateral parallel cousins are always the closest kin beyond the range of prohibited spouses. They appear to be conceptualised as the nearest collaterals even when marriages with them are not preferred.

From a Maronite Christian village in Lebanon, Peters reports first and second matrilateral parallel cousin marriages, patrilateral and matrilateral cross-cousin marriages of the first and second degree and other distant kin marriages. First patrilateral parallel cousin marriage is absent except for one extant case (Peters 1976: 61–2). Permission of a Church authority is necessary for any marriage. The cost of dispensation varies, from a trifling amount if there is no relationship, to a few pounds if the spouses are second matrilateral parallel cousins, and to fifty pounds or so if the spouses are first patrilateral parallel cousins. The closer the degree of consanguinity, the more elevated is the Church authority required to deal with it, first patrilateral parallel cousin marriage requiring the bishop's dispensation (ibid.: 48). Both the cost of dispensation and the level of Church authority from which permission is required clearly indicate that patrilateral parallel cousins are considered to be closer in degree of consanguinity than other cousins. The same idea has been reported from a Muslim village in Lebanon (Fuller 1961: 53)

Marriages between first patrilateral parallel cousins are followed in order of preference by marriages between classificatory patrilateral parallel cousins when agnation is emphasised over cognation in the evaluation of kinship distance (Marri Baluch, Baggara, Āl Murrah), and by marriages between other first cousins when cognation is stressed over agnation (Berti).

It has to be noted that many societies in the Middle East express a general preference for marriages between kin as opposed to marriages between strangers, without apparently differentiating between particular cousins. In Iran, there is a strong preference for marriages with cousins among both Muslims and Zoroatrians, but no particular type of cousin seems to be favoured over others (Tapper and Tapper 1988). For example, the Komachi in Kernan Province express a strong preference for marriages with close kin who are generally construed to be kin no more distant than one's second cousins, and they explicitly deny any preference for marriage with patrilateral parallel cousins (Bradburd 1984: 740–1). The Dhund in Pakistan similarly express a general preference for marriage with kinsmen (Donnan 1985: 183), without apparently favouring any particular cousin. The preference for FBD marriage is a more specific notion than this general preference for close kin marriages: it is a specific preference for marriage with the closest possible kin beyond the prohibited degrees.

My suggestion that preference for FBD marriages is a particular expression of a notion of higher generality – that of preference for marriages between close kin – goes further than that made by Goldberg (1967), for it assumes applicability not only where lineage organisation is unimportant but also where it is important (Marri Baluch, Baggara, Āl Murrah). It also goes further than the hypothesis formulated by Murphy and Kasdan (1959), for it does not see the preference for FBD marriages as necessarily logically correlated with the overriding importance ascribed to agnation (Berti). It is not challenged by the computer simulation and mathematical model devised by Gilbert and Hammel to test the validity of the hypothesis that high rates of FBD marriage can derive from preferences other than a specific one in favour of FBD. Interpreting the results of their analysis, Gilbert and Hammel allow for the possibility that an 'internally undifferentiated kinship preference for marrying a "close relative"' would account for the observed frequency of FBD marriage (1966: 89).

This conclusion is also confirmed by Randolph and Coult's computer analysis of the marriages of the Hawaashleh Bedouin of the Negev desert, which clearly shows a higher frequency of marriages between the members of agnatic groups the lower the level of their segmentation. If the observed marriage pattern were merely the result of the preference for lineage endogamy rather than the preference for marriages between close kin, more marriages between members of lineages of higher levels of segmentation should have occurred, since more marriageable women would be available to male members of these segments than to members of lower-order segments (Randolph and Coult 1968: 92–4).

When hypothesising that preference for FBD marriages is a particular expression of preference for marriages between close kin, I do not want to suggest that the actors themselves cannot formulate their preference as being for marriages within the lineage – the Baggara do. What I suggest, however, is that the preference is expressed in this way only when the primacy ascribed to agnation in computing kinship closeness has as its concomitant the cultural constitution of a definable category of agnates as the category of closest kin. When this is not the case, as among the Berti, in spite of the existence of lineages, the preference is not expressed as one for marriage within the lineage.

This point is of considerable significance in relation to the more general problem of interpretation in social anthropology and the role which interpretation plays in shaping anthropologists' explanatory strategies.

Meaning, interpretation and explanation

It has recently been acknowledged that the interpretation of a people's culture in the sense of properly identifying the meaning of specific cultural phenomena is a precondition of the explanation of these phenomena in the sense of elucidating the reasons for their existence. In this connection, Ortner and Whitehead suggest that 'one of the persistent problems of social anthropology ... has been, that in the rush to connect "culture" to "society", analysts have often taken culture in bits ..., nailing each bit to some specific feature of social organization ... without going through the crucial intervening phase of analyzing what that bit means' (1981: 4). I fully subscribe to this view that it is the lack of importance ascribed to the interpretation of the cultural phenomena within the overall strategy of their explanation which is responsible for the failure of many attempts at relating 'culture' to 'society'. I am, however, inclined to see the main problem of social anthropology somewhat differently.

In my view, this problem is not the neglect of interpretation or the neglect of the meaning of the studied phenomena as such. Either as human beings or as anthropologists, we cannot avoid interpretation any more than we can avoid speaking or writing in symbols. Identifying the problem in the way Ortner and Whitehead do seems to me to be a function of the recent recognition of two distinct traditions in social anthropology. The shift from one to the other, first manifest in the work of Evans-Pritchard and conceptualised as a shift from the analysis and explanation of social and cultural phenomena in terms of their functions to analysis and explanation in terms of their meanings (Pocock 1971: 72), has been hailed by some as a major epistemological shift in anthropology (Ardener 1971; Crick 1976; Comaroff 1980). I want to argue differently and suggest that the preoccupation with the study of meaning in contemporary anthropology can hardly be seen as a dramatic change in our epistemology. On the contrary, a distinct epistemological and methodological continuity exists between the two traditions.

The basic tenet of the anthropological study of meaning which is inspired by formal semantics and grounded in the linguistic model of culture is that the meaning of social and cultural phenomena is contextual, in the sense that it derives from the relationship to other phenomena within a particular systemic context. It is precisely this emphasis on context which keeps the semantically-informed study of meaning methodologically in company with orthodox functionalism, whose basic methodological tenet is that social and cultural phenomena must be analysed in the context of the total system of which they are part. Different conceptualisations of what precisely constitutes the systemic context of the studied phenomena reflect the ontological differences between the anthropologists explicitly interested in the study of meaning and their more orthodox colleagues; but a methodological and epistemological agreement underlies this ontological difference.

Parkin argues similarly that the alleged epistemological break has been 'less a sharp break and more a slide recognised after its occurence' (1982: xv; see also Barnes 1985: 9) and that 'the route has in fact been unbroken and is embraced by a single epistemology' (Parkin 1982: xvi). He suggests that a gradual transition rather than a clear break is also indicated 'in the analytical transformations surrounding the word "function" itself' (ibid.: v). The continuity is probably even more strongly suggested by the overlap in the senses of the words 'function' and 'meaning' (Holy and Stuchlik 1983: 28–9).

This has been recognised by Abercrombie (1980), who argues that the alternative approach to the received orthodoxy is nothing more than an 'ideological functionalism'. As meaning is the product of interpretation, it would be equally possible to argue that the accounts of social and cultural phenomena formulated by orthodox approaches in anthropology were as much concerned with the elucidation of their meaning as are the analyses of many semantic anthropologists. Indeed Comaroff, who expressly contrasts his own approach to the orthodox approaches, is able to say of the latter (in the context of the discussion of the meaning of marriage payments): 'For Goody, it is the nature of enduring social and economic structure, not the commercial logic of conjugal transactions, which gives form and *meaning* to these payments' (1980: 7, emphasis added). For Comaroff himself, their meaning derives from the 'constitutive relationship between the payment and the other elements of the socio-cultural system in which they occur' (ibid.). In the way it appears to be formulated, the difference between the anthropology specifically concerned with the study of meaning and the more orthodox approaches does not lie so much in the shift from interpretation in terms of function to interpretation in terms of meaning, as in a difference of opinion about which context should be seized upon in the construction of the explanation. On the one hand, this is the context of surface forms and processes of everyday life, of 'lived-in' order, of the enduring social and economic structures, or simply the context of social action; on the other hand, it is the context of the constitutive, organisational or structural principles which underlie the 'lived-in' universe, of the categories of the socio-cultural order, of an ordered set of values in any socio-cultural system or, briefly, the context of the symbolic system of culture.

As part of the context of social action, function is equated with instrumentality; as part of the context of the cultural or symbolic order, meaning is equated with symbolic expression: the meaning of a phenomenon lies in what the phenomenon 'says', what it expresses. Every phenomenon, be it an act, object, value, idea or whatever, pertains of course to both the domain of social action and the domain of the symbolic system which is culture, and it can be perceived, interpreted and evaluated in the context of both these domains. Once this is realised, the break involved in the shift of interest from function to meaning simply becomes a shift from concern with the system of social action (society, social structure) to concern with the symbolic system (culture) as the relevant context within which the studied phenomena are to be interpreted and explained.

What underlies both approaches is a decontextualisation of the phenomena in the process of their explanation. Each approach not only emphasises one of the two possible contexts within which the phenomenon can be placed to be understood but also brackets off the other one in the process of explanation. Here the interpretative work of the analysts parts way with the interpretative work of the actors, who habitually interpret and evaluate each phenomenon within both contexts. There are of course good reasons for that: the actors' interest in their own society and culture is practical; the anthropologists' interest is theoretical. This is frequently invoked as justification for the necessary differences between the actors' and analysts' interpretative work. It is, however, doubtful whether such a justification can hold. The actors' interpretative work is part of the reality which they perpetually construct and reconstruct through their practical accomplishments, including their interpretation of the world they live in. Once their interpretation of the phenomena is disregarded in our analyses, in which we interpret them according to our and not their criteria of contextual relevance, the studied reality is inevitably changed in the process.

The basic notion underlying the preoccupation of contemporary anthropology with meaning is that the meanings of social and cultural phenomena derive from their relations to other phenomena within the overall cultural context. In my view, the main drawback of this formal analysis of meaning lies in its treatment of culture (the surface forms) not as a speech but as a text, i.e. a closed system of utterances. Just as a sentence within a text can be interpreted as having a single particular meaning, *the* meaning of a phenomenon is what we end up with in this kind of analysis. But this procedure is misleading:

The sociology of thought is often cast in the role of a Hegelian observer able to understand and penetrate the dialectic of consciousness from a standpoint unavailable to its owners. There is a sense in which at its best it can have this kind of role. But if what is implied is that meanings can be detected in a cultural form of thought and action which are neither known nor given to it by anyone, at any level of consciousness or reflectiveness, present or past, *in* the culture concerned, then the enterprise is confused. Symbolic meaning presupposes a symbolic intelligence, and "consciousness", "mind", "conscience" or whatever cannot be personified independently of those whose consciousness it is, in order to play this part (Skorupski 1976: 48).

This procedure, habitually adopted in our analysis of meaning, blatantly contradicts our everyday experience, which shows that different phenomena have different meanings for different people, depending not only on their different conceptualisations of context but also on their own immediate intentions and purposes. Although formal analysis subscribes to the view that there is a dialectical relationship between surface processes and the organisational principles which underlie them, in practice the underlying principles are treated as generating the surface forms and processes.

The assumption of the dialectical relationship can be truly put into operation in our analyses only when we take seriously the obvious truism that context itself does not render a phenomenon meaningful, and when we put due emphasis on the fact – more often tacitly acknowledged than explicitly reflected in analysis – that meaning is the product of human consciousness: the product, that is, of cognition and reflective understanding deriving from the conscious interpretation of a phenomenon within a specific context. The notion of meaning is thus inseparable from that of the conscious agent. If we accept that meaning exists only in so far as it is the product of a reflective interpretation by a cognising subject, and if we retain the idea that the meaning of any phenomenon can be formulated only by cognising it in its relation to other phenomena within a specific context, it then follows that the meaning of any phenomenon is variable along two main dimensions. Firstly, it varies according to the identity of the cognising subject, since the same thing can have different meanings for different people. Secondly, the meaning varies according to its context, since the same item may have different meanings in different contexts (Milton 1982). These two dimensions of variation are intrinsically interdependent, for they issue from the same source. The contextual variation of a phenomenon's meaning also derives from the activity of the conscious subject, who discriminates between different contexts. In the last analysis, it is neither the phenomenon itself nor its context which is the source of possible variation in meaning, but only the activity of the conscious subject in his or her interpretation of these factors.

The main problem of anthropological inquiry stems from the involvement of two categories of cognising subjects in the production of the meanings of social and cultural phenomena: the analysts and the native actors. This, of course, is the problem of any social science, but it is particularly aggravated in social-anthropological studies by the fact that the analysts and native actors are usually members of different cultures. The probability that they will disagree about meaning is much greater than it would be if they were members of a single culture.

If the meaning of a phenomenon is understood to derive solely from its relationship to other phenomena within some encompassing system, then most modern anthropology can be said to be preoccupied with the 'meaning' of social and cultural phenomena (Parkin 1982: xvi), even if, until recently, this preoccupation has not expressly been acknowledged. The very essence of anthropological inquiry can be said to consist in the conscious attempt to render 'meaningful' the beliefs, customs and institutions of other cultures by showing their place within an integrated encompassing system. Two types of 'meaning' must be distinguished clearly, much as two types of function (latent and manifest) were distinguished before. So long as the cognitive endeavour of the actors is either explicitly or implicitly disregarded, the meaning ascribed to the studied phenomena is no more than a product of the reflective consciousness of the analyst. This type of meaning should properly be called 'sociological' (Meeker 1976: 257) or 'analytical'. It closely parallels the notion of a latent function in that both the latent function and this type of meaning are formulated by the analyst on the basis of *his* or *her* understanding of the contextual relevance. In contradistinction to this, 'cultural meaning' is produced by the reflective consciousness of the actors. It again closely parallels the notion of a manifest function in that both the manifest function and this type of meaning are cognised by the actors themselves. Obviously, analytical and cultural meanings will diverge when the analyst situates a studied phenomenon in a context different from that in which the actors habitually situate it. Such discrepancies have consequences for anthropological analyses which have been only partially recognised.

If the anthropologists endow a studied phenomenon with their own analytical meaning – that is, if they interpret the events and beliefs, and the customs and institutions of an alien culture in terms of their own criteria of discrimination, ones different from those of the culture under study – they do more than simply ignore the cultural meaning of the studied phenomenon. It has to be realised that when we ascribe meaning to phenomena, we do much more than make sense of them. These phenomena do not in any sense exist without being meaningful; through ascribing any particualr meaning to them, we in fact constitute them as such. When the anthropologists endow a studied phenomenon with their own analytical meaning, they inevitably change the object of their interest by conceptualising it in the way they do; or, put another way, they themselves create an object of study which has not had any existence prior to their analysis. In my view, the preference for lineage endogamy as an object of anthropological interest was crated precisely in this way.

The persistent problem of social anthropology is thus not the neglect of interpretation of the studied phenomena: interpretation is unavoidable in principle as no phenomenon can be contemplated independently of or prior to its interpretation, and anthropologists have been constantly interpreting the phenomena they study. Likewise, neglect of the meaning of the studied phenomena as such is not a persistent problem. For again, meaning cannot be neglected in principle since it is ontologically inseparable from the existence of the phenomenon as such. The persistent problem lies in treating the interpretation – i.e. the ascription of meaning to the phenomenon and, consequently, the proper identification of the phenomenon – as non-problematic. Instead of asking what the phenomenon means in the given social and cultural context, it is assumed that we know what it means in the first place (Ortner and Whitehead 1981: 1). We know what it means, of course because we have endowed it with our own meaning.

The tendency to build a theory from the ascription of meaning to phenomena in terms of criteria of discrimination different from the actors' own criteria has yet another important consequence for our understanding of the social and cultural reality which we study. When the analysts themselves define the context within which a phenomenon acquires its meaning, they also decide the relative importance of that specific context within the wider context of the whole culture. In other words, they not only explicitly define the meaning of the specific phenomenon which is the object of their analytical interest but also implicitly decide the significance of the context within which they situate the studied phenomenon. The ascription of analytical meaning to a specific social and cultural phenomenon thus has far-reaching consequences for the overall conceptualisation of the constitutive elements of a socio-cultural system and of their relative significance within the system. In the case of the interpretation of the preference for FBD marriages as an expression of lineage endogamy, one such consequence was that many societies, whose members do not necessarily ascribe corporateness to those related through agnatic kinship, were nevertheless credited with corporations, as Peters has rightly reminded us (1976: 32). The ultimate consequence of this procedure has been that most of our overall conceptualisation of the constitutive elements of the Middle Eastern socio-cultural system and of their relative significance within that system has not been derived from ethnography (and from the cultural meaning of facts constituting this ethnography) but generated by our epistemological assumptions. This is also strongly suggested by the fact that all recent studies, while admitting to the strength of agnatic ideology, point out the significance of dyadic relations and bilateral personal networks, emphasise the importance of sibling groups and stress the non-corporate nature of kin ties (e.g. Rosen 1972; Maher 1974; Geertz 1979; Eickelman 1976, 1981; Abu-Zahra 1976; Bourdieu 1977; Larson 1983).

The meaning of the preference for marriages between patrilateral parallel cousins, with which I have specifically been concerned in this chapter, parallels closely the descriptive, propositional or conceptual meaning of words and sentences which is the main object of study of formal linguistic semantics. Although this kind of meaning is differently theorised by different linguists, all formal semantics is concerned with specifying the sense of words and the propositional content of sentences in natural languages through analysing formally the structure of the language.

In the following chapters, I shall pay attention to another aspect of the meaning of the preference for FBD marriages. It is a meaning which parallels the meaning of utterances rather than words and sentences, and which most linguists consider to be within the domain of pragmatics because it is not determined by the syntactic or grammatical structure alone but derives from the context in which the utterance is produced. In other words, it is a meaning the formulation of which depends on the proper contextual interpretation. For this reason, I shall concentrate on discussing the contexts within which FBD marriages are interpreted by the actors, considering them first as instrumental acts which derive their significance from what may be broadly called the socio-structural context or the context of social action (Chapter 2), and later as expressive acts which derive their meaning from the cultural context (Chapters 3 and 4).

Unlike the linguists, the anthropologists interested in the study of meaning have concentrated almost exlusively on the situational, context-dependent meaning of social and cultural phenomena. Given this preoccupation, it may seem trivial to argue, as I have done in this chapter, that the preference for FBD marriages should be understood in the context of culturally-expressed preferences for marriages between close kin rather than as a preference for lineage endogamy. It may seem trivial because the elucidation of the cultural meaning of the expressed preference does not in itself provide an explanation for its existence, just as the elucidation of what someone uttered does not in itself provide an explanation for why he uttered it. The linguists have recognised that 'the study of meaning-in-context is logically subsequent to the study of semantic competence' (Leech 1981: 69) or of 'meaning-in-abstraction' (ibid.: 341), or at least that 'word-meaning and grammatical meaning of an utterance – both of which are encoded in the verbal component' are as relevant to the determination of the meaning of an utterance as are its non-verbal features (Lyons 1981: 26). The anthropologist needs equally to recognise that properly 'translating' a phenomenon or rendering it under its correct description is a necessary precondition for determining its context-dependent meaning. In this respect, the interpretation of the preference for FBD as a preference for the closest possible kinswoman beyond the prohibited range is the first necessary step in the overall explanatory strategy, in the same way that 'elucidating the meaning of what someone said must be a first step in explaining how what was said might have come to have the meaning it does, and why the person involved should have said it' (Skorupski 1976: 51).

The interpretation of the meaning of the preference for marriages between patrilateral parallel cousins, i.e. the understanding of what the actors have in mind when they assert that marriages between the children of two brothers are good and desirable or even the best of all marriages, can only be achieved by making sense of the expressed preference in terms of other cultural notions, conceptions, classifications and assumptions. The cultural conceptualisation of kinship and marriage, and in particular the classification of marriages according to their desirability and the classification of kinsmen according to the degree of closeness, appear to be the most important notions which endow the expressed preference with its cultural meaning as a preference for marrige between the closest possible kin beyond the prohibited range.

Elucidation of this meaning prior to the explanation of the reasons for the existence of the expressed preferences should not only ensure that the explanandum does not get changed in the process of explanation by being endowed with meaning different from that which it has for the actors themselves. It should also indicate which other cultural notions and which aspects of social relations will prove most significant in explaining the reasons for the existence of the expressed preference. In this respect, grasping the cultural meaning of the expressed preference is a precondition for any understanding of the reasons the actors themselves have for holding it, for a phenomenon has to be grasped 'under its correct description before the actor's own literalising rationalisation of it can be explained' (Skorupski 1976: 43).

Notes to Chapter 1

1 Pitt-Rivers (1977: 162–3) and Goody (1983: 31) also point out that, strictly speaking, Arab clans and lineages are not endogamous if endogamy is understood as the opposite of exogamy.
2 Analyses of Middle Eastern marriage systems in terms of the theory of exchange relationships developed by Lévi-Strauss are virtually non-existent. A notable exception is Cuisenier, who interprets the Arab marriage system as a system of exchanges down to the level of brothers (1962: 104). For a criticism of the structuralist approach see Chelhod 1964, and for a discussion of the difficulties posed by FBD marriage to both descent and alliance theory see Barnard and Good 1984: 166.
3 Salim 1962: 47–8; Stirling 1965: 154; Cunnison 1966: 111; Lutfiyya 1966: 144; Marx 1967: 223; Asad 1970: 104; Antoun 1972: 70; Geertz 1979: 347–8; R. Tapper 1979: 126; Abu-Lughod 1986: 56.
4 Granqvist 1931: 87; Davies 1949: 250; Patai 1955; 1962: chapter 6; Peters 1960: 44; 1980: 137; Lutfiyya 1966: 129; Antoun 1972: 125; R. Tapper 1979: 140–1; Cole 1984: 179; Nassehi-Behnam 1985: 558.
5 Useful figures are provided by Granqvist 1931: 81–2; Barth 1954: 167, 169; Barclay 1964: 120; Randolph and Coult 1968: 88–90; Khuri 1970: 559; Bates 1973: 65–6; Holy 1974: 72–5; Keyser 1974: 297; Irons 1975: 129–30; Fischer 1978: 211; Pastner 1979: 36–43; 1981: 313; 1986: 577; R. Tapper 1979: 142; McCabe 1983: 62; Bradburd 1984: 741.
6 A notable exception is R. Tapper, who pays specific analytical attention to the higher occurrence of MBD–FZS than FBD–FBS marriages among the Shahsevan nomads of north-western Iran (R. Tapper 1979: 142–4).
7 Similar sayings have been reported from Morocco: 'people like to marry the daughter of their paternal uncle, just as they like to eat meat of their own breeding' (literally: slaughter an animal from their herd) (Tillion 1983: 74); 'he who marries the daughter of his father's brother is like him who celebrates his feast with a sheep from his own flocks' (Eickelman 1981: 129; Webster 1982: 170).
8 This kind of relationship classification can be found elsewhere in the Middle East. For example, Bates notes that among the Yörük, 'when marriages cut across lineage lines or tribal identities, the emergent linkages of close consanguinity are not systematically obscured by more distant or putative relationships through common agnatic descent' (1973: 64). Regrettably, he does not provide information on whether among the Yörük marriages between first cousins other than FBD–FBS are preferred over marriages with classificatory patrilateral parallel cousins or vice versa.

In many cases, the tracing of the relationship between spouses as that of agnatic rather than non-agnatic kinship, particularly if the relationship among them is a distant one, is simply a function of the fact that fewer maternal than paternal ascendants are remembered and mentioned in genealogies, or of tracing kinship links much farther through the male than the female line (cf. Randolph and Coult 1968: 85; Irons 1975: 129). The genealogical connection can also be traced differently by men and by women. Bourdieu notes that the way of tracing genealogical connections may be determined by context and he points out that the official way, employed by men, emphasises links through men, whereas the unofficial way, employed by women, is through the more direct female links (1977: 41–2).

9 Although Cole stresses the importance of affinal and matrilateral links among them in his 1984 paper, in his 1975 book he gives a distinct impression of the overriding importance of agnation: the terms for close agnates are extended to all who are agnatically related, however removed the relationship, whereas cognatic terms are not thus extended (1975: 83–5); mother's brothers and sisters, 'according to Āl Murrah notions of patrilineality, are not blood kinspeople but relatives through marriage' (1975: 73).

10 In some villages it is said to be even higher and to range around 60 per cent (Barth 1953: 27). These figures are suspect. Such high occurence of marriages with first cousins would require extremely large families producing many cousins who are potential marriage partners (see Marx 1967: 226) and this does not seem to be the case (Barth 1953: 19, table 1).

Chapter 2

Pragmatic functions of FBD marriages and the marriage pattern

Most analyses of preferential marriages in the Middle East have concentrated on the explanation of the observable marriage pattern. They have typically been concerned with two issues: the formulation of possible reasons for the occurrence of preferential marriages in terms of actors' strategies, reasons and motivations, and the analysis of their consequences for the structure of social relations in the societies in which preferential marriages are practised. It is generally the case in anthropological theorising that these two types of inquiry are seen as yielding answers to the same problem, and in consequence it is assumed that one somehow subsumes the other or makes the other superfluous or redundant. This kind of reasoning is particularly prominent in those approaches which assume that the consequences of a certain practice also provide adequate reasons for its existence (a kind of explanation which Homans and Schneider (1955) called a 'final cause theory').

Marriage strategies and the marriage pattern

The consequence of a certain practice is a specific pattern of social relations. As the actors do not strategise in a vacuum but within a specific pattern of social relations, this pattern itself is a factor which they take into account when making strategic decisions. Thus it is possible that the consequences of a certain practice can become the reasons for the actors' perpetuation of this practice, and one can argue that the consequences of a particular practice and the reasons for its adoption, existence or perpetuation are the same. It is possible to argue thus, however, only if it can be shown that the actors consciously link a specific pattern of social relations to a certain practice or see the existing pattern as resulting from it. But this is usually impossible to do (Heath 1976), and as long as this is the case, equating the consequences of a certain practice with the reasons for its adoption or existence can be done only at the expense of reifying the social structure.

To a great extent, the discussion of preferential marriages in the Middle East has remained free of this methodological error, so common in most anthropological discussions. Murphy and Kasdan (1959) make a clear distinction between the reasons for men marrying their FBDs and the consequences of this type of marriage, and concern themselves with the consequences. Whether the reasons for men marrying their FBDs are consolidation of wealth or of power, the consequence (or 'structural function' in Murphy and Kasdan's terminology) of this type of marriage is that it turns affinal bonds inward, making each minimal-sized agnatic unit virtually self-contained and encysted (cf. also Kaplan 1973: 567). The preferential marriage with FBD promotes the extreme fission of agnatic lines and inhibits the formation of corporate groups on higher levels of segmentation, leaving the genealogies as the only means of ordering relations between and within agnatic sections.

Like Murphy and Kasdan, Barth also draws a clear distinction between the reasons for the existence of the patrilateral parallel cousin marriage and its consequences. He sees the latter differently from Murphy and Kasdan. In his earlier paper he saw the main consequences of the parallel cousin marriage 'in solidifying the minimal lineage as a corporate group in factional struggle' (Barth 1954: 171). In his later paper he saw as the main consequences of this type of marriage that kinship and affinal relations become regarded as essentially 'of the same kind', and that the opposed units in confrontations involving related parties 'are not unilineal descent segments but *factions*, built on bilateral and affinal relations, friendship and opportunistic alliances as well as a selection of agnatic relations' (Barth 1973: 12, 13, 17).

In this chapter, I am not specifically concerned with the consequences of the preference for FBD marriages for the social structure of Middle Eastern societies. My concern is with the analysis of the reasons for which marriages between patrilateral parallel cousins are positively valued throughout the area and for which the actors themselves assert a preference for them.

Preference for FBD marriage and the marriage pattern

As it has been quite rightly felt that people do not marry as they do simply because they prefer certain types of marriages to others, but because certain marriages have strategic advantages, the strategy for explaining FBD marriage has for the most part concentrated on identifying the pragmatic reasons which motivate this practice; the implication is that the ideologically-asserted preference for FBD marriage is thus accounted for. The methodological problems involved in this explanatory strategy are both general and specific. The general problem derives from the fact that it is a strategy guided by an attempt to postulate an immediate connection between a particular culture and a particular social structure, which, as it were, jumps the gun by aiming at an explanation before properly identifying the phenomenon to be explained.

There is a failure in such accounts to understand that culture itself has the properties of a system, a system that mediates between any given symbol and its social grounding. The meaning of specific cultural features is as much a function of their fit within a wider symbolic context as it is of their relevance to (or reference to) a particular social institution, and serious interpretive distortions may arise when this wider cultural context is slighted in favor of a quick Durkheimian fix (Ortner and Whitehead 1981: 4).

The analytical procedure criticised here derives from the view of culture as a reflection of the structure of social relations. On this view, the function of culture is to express, maintain or reinforce that structure. Obviously, when the same cultural feature, such as the preference for FBD marriage, is found among different and greatly variable structures of social (or economic or political) relations, the 'quick Durkheimian fix' fails and the functional fit of the marriage preference with the underlying or accompanying structure becomes impossible to establish.

One particular result of favouring this 'quick Durkheimian fix' is the underlying assumption that the observable marriage pattern and the ideologically-asserted preference are generated by the same practical concerns of the actors. As long as we are able correctly to pinpoint these concerns, we explain, at the same time, both the observable marriage pattern and the asserted preference. While I would subscribe to the view that the actors' choices are motivated by their practical concerns and that the observable marriage pattern is thus their outcome or, more generally, that the social structure is best seen as the outcome of the multiplicity of individual choices (Leach 1960: 124), I do not subscribe to the view that the actors' ideals and the existing cultural rules are generated by the same pragmatic reasons as their observable behaviour. Such a view plunges us into the fallacy of assuming practical motivation for the existing culture: the culture of a society is simply treated as the epiphenomenon of the practical concerns of its members.

This kind of reasoning is possible only if the relation between the culturally-asserted preference and the behavioural practice is treated as non-problematic, and if the possible meaning of the preference within the context of the culture of which it is a part is disregarded and only its meaning in the context of the pattern of social action is considered. As the postulated pragmatic reasons for marrying patrilateral cousins, or functions (whether manifest or latent) of this type of marriage, differ from society to society, the preferential patrilateral cousin marriage is inevitably seen either as sociologically inexplicable or, on the basis of the numerical prevalence of other types of marriages, as insignificant within the overall marriage pattern and hence not worthy of special attention. It is declared a curiosity (Antoun 1976: 166; cf. Eickelman 1981: 134) which is not worthy of the interest of the anthropologist, whose mind would be better occupied by solving other more relevant problems concerning the Middle Eastern marriage pattern.

I have alluded to some of these general methodological problems before. In this chapter I want to pay attention to some of the specific problems which this explanatory strategy does not seem to have adequately resolved. I use the reasons invoked by the Berti for marriages between close kin, and their reasons for preferring such marriages to those with strangers, as an ethnographic background against which some of these problems can best be discussed.

Berti marriage preferences

Two views about marriage preferences are discernible among the Berti: one, shared by both men and women, according to which marriages between kinsmen are preferable to those between strangers; and the other, expressed by men, according to which marriages between closest marriageable kin, i.e. patrilateral parallel cousins, are preferable to any others. This would seem to indicate that, while the same meaning is ascribed to marriage by both men and women, marriage has also a specific meaning for men which is not shared by the women. If we accept that the meaning of an act derives from the context in which it is seen, it would also indicate that, whilst both men and women evaluate marriages in a context which is significant to both of them, men evaluate them also in a context which is significant only to them.

The difference of views between men and women on the relative significance of the various contexts within which marriages acquire their meanings derives also from the fact that a woman is under the authority of her husband and that it is men who conduct all formal marriage negotiations. If the wife's opinion about the marriage of their child differs from that of her husband, she cannot reveal it publicly but must formally submit to his opinion. But in spite of this, a woman often succeeds in having her children married according to her own wishes, even if she has to resort to secret negotiations with her own kinsmen and kinswomen and often to complicated intrigues and subterfuge.

For both men and women, the whole socio-cultural reality represents, in a sense, the context in which their marriage preferences are embedded.

When evaluating some marriages as preferable to others, or judging the desirability of particular matches, they refer, however, to specific aspects of this reality. Each such aspect is the immediate context in which the marriages brought into contrast on the basis of their specific discriminating features are evaluated.

The contexts within which marriages are evaluated are clearly indicated by the reasons which the Berti give for their assertions that certain marriages are better than others. They see marriages between kinsmen as preferable because of their positive effect on relations between spouses, because of their distinct economic and political advantages and because they are easier to negotiate and arrange than marriages between strangers.

Relations between spouses

The Berti expect that marital relations will be harmonious and cooperative if the spouses are related. Although this is advantageous for both spouses, when arguments about the desirability of a particular marriage arise, harmonious relations and mutual loyalty between spouses are more often presented as benefiting primarily the husband rather than the wife. This is quite understandable if we take into account the fact that a man has greater freedom than a woman to assert his views about the prospective marriage, which his father tries to arrange for him. Whatever the father's reasons are for arranging a particular marriage for his son, he has to persuade him that such a marriage is primarily to his own advantage; there is not such a strong need to persuade his daughter about the advantage of her prospective marriage, for she has less opportunity to assert her own views about it. No doubt, the expected benefits accruing to a man who marries his kinswoman can, in many cases, be the genuine reasons for contracting a particular kind of marriage; in other words the man's father or marriage guardian arranges a particular marriage for him, motivated by a desire to secure for him a distinct advantage. In other cases, however, the advantages accruing to the husband are a legitimisation for a particular marriage which was primarily contracted because of its envisaged benefits for the man's father, parents or marriage guardian.

The Berti give a number of specific reasons why a marriage between kin is to the husband's advantage.

They say *az zōl kān bākhud, bākhud wilian* ('when a man marries, he marries the guardians'). The implication of this saying is that a man is not as much concerned with the character of his prospective bride as with the character of her guardian (*wali*, pl. *wilian*), who is typically her father; when choosing a wife for himself, one of the man's most important considerations is thus who his father-in-law will be. This is quite understandable given the rigidity of the relationship between the father-in-law and the son-in-law, which is particularly observed during the first years of marriage when the wife still lives in her parents' household and her husband visits her there periodically. As he cannot eat in his father-in-law's presence until he is expressly invited to do so, he is effectively debarred from enjoying the hospitality and its accompanying sociability which will, as a matter of course, be offered to any other visitor. He has his own shelter in his parents-in-law's household, in which he stays alone and eats alone while his wife associates with the members of her parents' household and their visitors. It is particularly harsh for him to stay in his leaking shelter on a rainy night when all other male visitors would be invited to stay in his father-in-law's hut, or during the cold nights in winter when everybody else enjoys the comfort of the warm fire inside the hut. He effectively avoids all these hardships if his father-in-law is his kinsman, for the less rigid pattern of behaviour between them will continue after his marriage.

This is by no means the only advantage which the marriage between kin has for the husband. When there are male visitors to the house, they are entertained by the household head but it is his wife who has to provide the food. She is expected to do it without being asked and it is considered shameful if the husband has to remind her of her duties in front of them. If they are her kinsmen, she will always provide the appropriate hospitality; she may be reluctant to do so, however, if the visitors are the husband's kinsmen. She will always be prepared to attend to her duties if her husband's kinsmen are at the same time her own. She will take care of them even if the husband is temporarily absent from the home, which would not be the case if they were not related to her. As with many other explicitly-stated advantages of marriages between kinsmen, what is to the husband's advantage is also to the advantage of his kinsmen. If his wife is also related to them, they can always rely on his hospitality and they know that they will be able to enjoy it even if he is temporarily absent from his house; this would not necessarily be the case if she were a stranger.

A wife who is related to her husband can be expected to be more loyal to him than a wife who is a stranger. In his old age or in case of illness or some other misfortune which befalls him, she will care for him and support him because he is not only her husband but first of all her kinsman. The Berti support their assertion that a wife who is a kinswoman is more loyal to her husband than a wife who is a stranger by narrating numerous stories about the devotion of wives who were their husbands' kinswomen: 'There was a fight between the Berti and the Meidob and one Berti man who was married to his FBD was stabbed by the knife by a Meidob and his abdomen was cut open. His wife wrapped a piece of cloth round his abdomen and she was herself fighting the Meidob with her husband's spear, running back to her husband and treating his wounds. She took her husband to the village and called other people to help. She would not have cared for him in this way if he was not her kinsman'.[1]

The Berti are realistic enough to expect that quarrels will occasionally erupt between husband and wife. If the dispute is a serious one, the wife will leave her husband and return to her parents or take refuge with one of her brothers or sisters. If this happens, the husband cannot expect her to come back by herself and he has to go and bring her back. This involves him invariably in negotiations with the kinsmen with whom she is staying. If she is not related to him, he has to deal with strangers who are likely to show very little sympathy for his point of view; he is more likely to have a sympathetic reception if his wife's kinsmen are at the same time his own. If the husband fails to try to bring his wife back or if his efforts to do so are unsuccessful, the dispute is referred to the elders, who try to reconcile the spouses and thus to prevent their marriage from breaking up. The elders call on the marriage guardians of both husband and wife; and if the couple are related, so are their guardians. The dispute becomes a dispute between kinsmen and as such has a better chance of being resolved for two reasons. Firstly, the value of kinship amity can be evoked, and the effort of both parties to the dispute to preserve amicable relations among themselves and to patch up their differences works automatically towards the reconciliation of the spouses. At stake is not only the dissolution of a particular marriage but a possible rift between kinsmen: the effort to avoid the latter automatically involves the prevention of the former. Secondly, the marriage guardian of the husband is at the same time a kinsman of the wife and vice versa. In this situation, each marriage guardian is less likely solely to back up one of the spouses against the accusations and claims of the other. His loyalties in the dispute are not unilateral but divided. Only the reconciliation of the dispute can prevent a conflict of loyalties for each marriage guardian; in consequence, both marriage guardians work hard towards it. At the same time, the fact that they are each related to both principal disputants makes the reconciliation not only desirable but also practically possible, for both guardians can put pressure not only on one of the spouses but on both of them.

The fact that a marriage between kinsmen has a better chance of surviving the crises of married life is not only to the advantage of the married couple: many of the advantages which their fathers or parents try to secure for themselves by arranging this kind of marriage can be achieved only if the marriage endures.

The marriage between kinsmen has advantages not only for the husband or for both spouses jointly. In the Berti's view, it is clearly also to the wife's particular advantage. The wife is fully under the authority of her husband, who has a right to beat her if she is disobedient. If she is his kinswoman, it can be expected that he will beat her less severely than if she were a stranger. As the Berti say of the husband who is also a kinsman: *Hu yākul lahamak, mā yaksur 'adumak* ('he eats your flesh but does not break your bone').

Economic aspects of marriage

Marriages between close kin are seen as being to the advantage not only of the married couple but also of their parents.

The viability of a Berti household pursuing a mixed agricultural and pastoral economy depends on the availability of labour. Various agricultural tasks like sowing, weeding, harvesting and threshing have to be performed simultaneously with various pastoral tasks like watering and herding the animals and with various tasks like drawing water, collecting firewood and preparing food and millet beer. A household which depends solely on the labour of a married couple faces severe organisational problems as far as allocation of labour is concerned, and it is the limited labour which impedes the accumulation of wealth in terms of livestock. These problems are alleviated when the children of the married couple become old enough to take part in production. A household towards the end of its stage of expansion has optimum labour available for performing all the various productive tasks, and it is typically at this stage that the family herd is systematically built up and pastoralism becomes an important part of the household's economy. Once the household enters the stage of its dispersal, with children gradually marrying out and establishing their own households, the parents' household starts losing labour which it has to replace if it is to maintain its viability, and it is now the labour of their grandchildren which the grandparents try to secure.

The ultimate authority over the children rests with the father, who alone has the right to decide whether his child will be lent to either his own or his wife's parents. Irrespective of who is the son's wife, his parents can acquire the labour of his child or children if he is prepared to assert his authority. His wife might, of course, object to having her children brought up outside her own household, and the son's loyalty to his parents may lead to a conflict with his wife. The danger of a marital conflict is reduced if the son is married to a kinswoman and thus at least one of his parents is also her close relative.

The daughter's marriage is of crucial importance from the point of view of acquiring the labour of her children. The ultimate authority over them rests with her husband, who will, naturally, favour his own parents unless at least one of his wife's parents is also his own relative. Thus, while it is good but not essential for the parents to marry their son to a kinswoman if they want to acquire for themselves the labour of his children, it is essential for them to marry their daughter to a kinsman if they want to acquire the labour of her children. The parent's strategic considerations relate positively to the fact that they can assert more strongly their right to choose the daughter's husband than their right to choose the son's wife. While it is rare for a man to be married without his knowledge or consent, and while his right to refuse a wife chosen for him by his father is usually recognised, a woman is quite often informed about her marriage only after it has been formally concluded. I have heard about several cases of suicide by women who did not want to be married to men chosen for them by their parents.

When considering the marriage of their children, the Berti do not aim merely at securing the labour of their grandchildren. One of their major considerations is to secure provision for their old age, when they will no longer be able to produce and prepare their own food.

Cooking and brewing beer is woman's work and it is very shameful for a man to engage in these tasks. As long as his marriage endures, it is his wife who prepares his daily food and millet beer. He becomes dependent on some other woman from the moment his wife dies or is divorced, even if he is himself still capable of taking an active part in production. A divorced or widowed woman is usually able to cook her own food and brew her own beer, even when she is no longer able to cultivate her field or to look after any livestock which she might still have or to supply her household with water and firewood. She is thus usually able to manage her own household longer than a man; but as she gets older and more infirm she also becomes more and more dependent on outside help. Both men and women expect their children to provide this help. Their children can do so, however, only if their spouses allow them to do so and only if they live nearby. Parents who aim at securing the help and support of their children in their old age have to arrange their marriages with this fact in mind. The strategic considerations of a man differ in this respect from those of his wife.

The Berti consider the support of his ageing father to be the son's jural obligation. Although I did not come across a single case of a father suing his son for neglect, all my informants insisted that a son who neglects his father would be taken to the court, which would enforce his obligations. Although a son can support his ageing father in many ways, for food and beer the father does not depend ultimately on his son but on his son's wife. The latter takes care of her father-in-law only because he is the father of her husband, to whose authority she is bound. This is not the case if her husband's father is also either her 'father' (FB) or her *khāl* (MB). A man's marriage to either his FBD or his FZD is thus an outcome of his father's strategy to secure provision for his old age.

The Berti do not agree among themselves whether it is more advantageous for a man to rely on the help and support of his son or of his daughter. Although they all agree that it is a son's obligation to support his father in his old age, some argue that a man will be better looked-after by his daughter. It is, after all, a woman who cooks and brews beer, they say, and if the father is looked after by his daughter, he can always be sure that he will not go hungry. A married woman is, however, under her husband's authority, and if the latter objects to using his household's produce for supporting his father-in-law, his wife can support her father only in secret and she runs a perpetual danger of being accused by her husband of stealing. He will not object to his wife's behaviour if her father is at the same time also his 'father' or his *khāl*. A daughter's marriage to either her FBS or her FZS is thus possibly again an outcome of her father's strategy to secure provision for his old age. A woman's marriage to her FZS is, of course, a marriage with his MBD from the point of view of her husband. Most marriages which could be classified as MBD marriages following the usually practice of classifying close cousin marriages from the man's point of view, are in fact better viewed as marriages of a woman to her FZS. As mentioned before, a man does not object to his wife supporting her father if the latter is also his FB or his *khāl*.

In his strategic considerations a man's relationship to his future son-in-law is thus of the utmost importance. Berti men differ in their respective evaluations of this relationship. A considerable number of them are of the opinion that a man will be better treated by his son-in-law if he is the latter's MB than if he is his FB. A BS's attachment to his FB derives from the normatively-asserted solidarity of close agnates, which is, however, perpetually threatened by the rivalry between them. Should the relationship between a man and his brother become strained, his effort to secure provision for his old age may to a great extent be frustrated if he married his daughter off to his brother's son. To avoid this danger, a considerable number of men prefer their daughter to be married to their sister's son. They argue that their sister's son will support them under all circumstances, not because of the normatively-stipulated obligation on his part but because of his genuine love and affection for his MB: 'The sister's son will never leave his mother's brother. If there is any danger, he will die together with him. When you become old, your sister's son will take care of you, and if your daughter does not treat you well, he may even beat her. If he has his house in another village, he will take you there to stay with him when you have become old'.

For reasons similar to those for which the father may prefer his ZS to his BS as his son-in-law, the son himself may prefer his MB to his FB as his father-in-law. Particularly in the early stages of his marriage, when his wife still lives in her parents' household, the informality of behaviour between the MB and the ZS affects the man's relationship with his father-in-law; as the behaviour between FB and BS is never so relaxed as that between MB and ZS, the relationship between a man and his father-in-law is always more rigid when the latter is his FB. Many MBD–FZS marriages are thus not only motivated by the strategic considerations of the bride's father but also by those of the bridegroom himself.

If a woman tries to secure the help and support of her children in her old age, the marriage of her children to those of her brother or sister will be her aim, in the same way as the marriage of his children to those of either his brother or sister is the man's main aim. A son's marriage to his MBD or his MZD and a daughter's marriage to her MBS (FZD marriage from the latter's point of view) or her MZS can thus be an outcome of their mother's strategy to secure provision for her old age.

As a rule, a woman is much more concerned with her daughter's marriage than with her son's, for, in her own economic activities, she depends on the continuous support of her daughter more than the support of her son. Furthermore, as virilocal residence is considered normal and ideal, it is expected that the son will build his household in the village of his parents irrespective of whom he marries, and that his economic cooperation with his parents will thus not be completely interrupted. The daughter's economic cooperation can be completely lost if she resides virilocally. Under the prevailing conditions of virilocal residence, the daughter's marriage to any cousin other than her FBS is likely to take her away from her parents' village. The question of post-marital residence enters more strongly into consideration of the daughter's than the son's marriage. While on the one hand a woman certainly prefers her daughter to be married to her own kinsman, on the other hand she does not want her to leave her own village. Should her marriage to a matrilateral cousin take her away, her mother herself may prefer her to be married to her FBS who lives in the same village and will thus establish his own household there. The marriage of the daughter to her FBS can then be not only her father's preference but is quite often also favoured by her mother. On the other hand, the mother may be prepared to put up with her daughter moving out of her own village if the daughter marries her own kinsman. She can then at least visit her frequently and her visits are free from tension and embarrassment if her daughter lives in the household of her brother or sister. Equally, her daughter's husband will not object to his wife visiting her mother frequently if the latter is also his FZ or MZ.

When the Berti try to secure for themselves various future economic services by properly arranging their children's marriages, their marriage strategies are grounded in their knowledge that these services will be provided because they ensue from the normative obligations people have towards one another as kinsmen and from the love and affection which obtains among them. They would not be provided if the parties were related merely as affines for two reasons. Firstly, the affines are not normatively compelled to cooperate to the same extent as the kinsmen are; and, secondly, the normative prescription of their conduct practically inhibits any effective provision of desirable services: for example, a daughter-in-law who is expected to avoid her father-in-law, as she is if the father of her husband is not her own kinsman, can hardly cater for him effectively, even if she wants to.

Considered in terms of their pragmatic functions, marriages between kinsmen are thus preferable to those between strangers because, unlike the latter, the only relations of affinity which they create are those between husband and wife. Only husband and wife stop using their former kinship terms in reference to one another and adopt instead the terms *um iyāli* – 'mother of my children' – and *abu iyāli* – 'father of my children', and only the husband's and wife's previous conduct is modified after marriage to a considerable extent. All other previously existing kinship relationships, with their concomitant rights and obligations, remain practically unaffected by the marriage. Any time a relationship is that of both kinship and affinity, the Berti treat it consistently as a kinship one: kinship terms which were used before marriage continue to be used after it and the conduct appropriate for the two kinship roles continues basically to be in force, or at least significantly modifies the conduct appropriate for the parallel affinal relationship. It is precisely because of this nullifying effect on the relations of affinity that marriages between kinsmen are preferred to those between strangers. In fact, the expectations of all the advantages ensuing from such marriages are predicated on the continuity of the previous behaviour of those who have been brought into a close affinal relationship.

For the Berti, this continuity is particularly important in the relationship between parents-in-law and children-in-law. This is most clearly shown in their evaluation of inter-generational marriages between kinsmen, some of which are marriages with either the father's or the mother's classificatory sister, but most of which are marriages with a classificatory daughter, i.e. marriages with the daughter of the first or more distant cousin. Unlike intra-generational marriages, such marriages are ambiguous. While some people maintain that they are good marriages because they are, after all, marriages between kinsmen, others are of the opinion that it is not a good thing to marry one's 'daughter' or father's or mother's sister, and on the scale of desirability they do not rank such marriages any higher than those between strangers. The reasons for this lie in the nature of the relationship between the parents-in-law and children-in-law which such marriages create.

In an intra-generational marriage the child-in-law is always a relative to whom the parents-in-law refer by the same kinship term as to their own child and over whom they hold similar rights. Consequently, the children-in-law have duties towards their parents-in-law similar to those towards their own parents. It is this close and at the same time asymmetrical relationship that guarantees the rendering of economic services which the parents try to secure for themselves through marrying their 'children' to one another. In inter-generational marriages, the children-in-law are either classificatory brothers or sisters (i.e. first or more distant cousins) or 'grandchildren'. In the first case, the relationship between parents-in-law and children-in-law is that of equality, which inhibits the desirable unidirectional flow of services. Moreover, it is a relationship of rivalry which crosses the first potential line of cleavage between collaterals and, in the degree of mutual solidarity implied in it, it is always superseded by the relationship between parents and children. A 'brother' or 'sister' always tends to support first of all his or her 'parents' and only after that his or her 'siblings'. In the second case, although the relationship between parents-in-law and children-in-law is an asymmetrical relationship of subordination and superordination, it is again a relationship which is superseded by the relationship between parents and children as far as the degree of mutual solidarity is concerned. While from the parents' point of view much can be gained economically through mutual marriages of their 'children', no special economic advantages ensue for them from marriages between kinsmen of different generations.

The Berti point out that, when seeking economic advantages for themselves through mutual marriages of their children, the strategic considerations of the two parents can differ and conflict with one another. They characterise the situation by saying that a man wants his child to be married to his own kin whereas a woman wants her child to be married to hers.[2]

Although marriages are formally negotiated by men, marriage arrangements are rarely discussed among them. They are, however, the most popular topic of conversation among women. Any time they chat among themselves, their conversation invariably turns, after a few minutes, to the discussion of past marriages, present marriage negotiations and possible future matches. In line with this general pattern, the father never talks with his children about their marriage; he is likely to bring up the issue of his son's marriage only when he informs him about the bride he has chosen for him or, more rarely, when he feels that the time has arrived for him to get married and mentions this to him. The mother, on the other hand, quite frequently discusses her son's prospective marriage with him and, in the course of these conversations, encourages him to marry either her brother's or her sister's daughter. While a daughter is fully under her father's authority and can be, and very often is, married not only against her will but without her consent or even knowledge, a son has more opportunity to express his own opinion about his marriage and in many cases win his way. His possible preference for his MBD to his FBD, which I mentioned before, can often well be the result of his mother's influence.

Although the Berti are certainly correct in their observation that the marriage strategies of a man and his wife often differ, the possible conflict of interest is in many cases avoided because the marriages between close kinsmen contracted in previous generations link the spouses through a multiplicity of connections, and consequently a son- or daughter-in-law is often closely related to both of his or her parents-in-law.

Political aspects of marriage

The expressed preference for marriages between kinsmen as against those between strangers derives from considering a marriage in two closely interrelated contexts: one is the context of specific economic relations; the other is the context of relations of kinship and affinity, in which the kinship relations are consistently valued over the relations of affinity. As these contexts are directly relevant to all Berti, both men and women express the view that marriages between kinsmen are better than those between strangers. The expressed preference for marriages between patrilateral parallel cousins derives from considering a marriage in two other contexts: one is the context of specific political relations; the other is the context of marriage negotiations. As these two contexts are of much greater significance to men than to women, it is primarily the men who express the view that marriage between patrilateral parallel cousins is better than any other marriage including that between more distant kinsmen. Parallel cousin marriage is thus 'a matter for men, consistent with the men's interests' (Bourdieu 1977: 64). These interests are, however, not only 'the higher interests of the lineage, often arranged without the women being informed, and *against their will*' (ibid.), but also the men's *individual* interests.

The marriage between patrilateral parallel cousins is considered to be of specific political significance, especially for the bride's father. By marrying his daughter to his brother's son a man increases, as the Berti express it, his lineage (*warrai*) or his progeny (*dor*). Not only his son's but also his daughter's children will be his close agnates, who, in case he has to pay compensation for killing, injury or damage to property (*diya*), will be under an obligation to contribute to it more substantially than both his close cognates and his more distant agnates. Obviously, a woman's children will be of the same lineage as their maternal grandfather, not only when she marries her FBS but also when she simply marries within her own lineage. However, if the genealogical relationship between the spouses is not close enough, the woman's children will not necessarily count as close agnates of their maternal grandfather, and in consequence the Berti do not see any particular advantage in a marriage within the lineage if there is no close genealogical connection between the spouses. When both political and economic aspects of the marriage are taken into consideration, a woman's marriage to a close kinsman of a different lineage is generally viewed as preferable to her marriage to a man from her own lineage to whom no close genealogical connection can be traced.

The pattern of marriage negotiations

The preference for marriages between patrilateral parallel cousins which the men express derives also from its significance within the context of marriage negotiations.

Although women have a considerable degree of informal say in the marriage arrangements of their children, and some of them are very skilful in manipulating them according to their own wishes, it is men who conduct all formal marriage negotiations. The degree of ease and informality with which a particular marriage can be arranged is an important consideration for them, because negotiating a marriage can often be a harrowing experience for the fathers of both the boy and the girl: it is a situation in which the strategic considerations of the interested parties are quite often mutually conflicting.

In the men's view, the marriage between patrilateral parallel cousins is the best, not only because of the practical advantages mentioned before but also because it is the easiest one to negotiate and arrange. In the case of marriages between cross-cousins or matrilateral parallel cousins, the fathers of the future spouses, who negotiate the match, are affines, provided that no kinship connection resulting from some previous intermarriage exists between them. The ease which accompanies the negotiation of marriage between patrilateral parallel cousins derives from the fact that of all possible marriages this is the only one in whose arrangements kinsmen alone are involved. Being brothers, the fathers of both spouses are equal in status and either of them can initiate the marriage negotiations. This is another factor which greatly contributes to the relaxed informality which characteristically accompanies arrangements of marriages between patrilateral parallel cousins. In any other type of marriage it is always the boy's father who is expected to suggest the marriage of his son to the father of the girl.

The next in order of the ease with which they can be arranged are the marriages between cross-cousins. When a man tries to arrange a marriage between his son and his sister's daughter, his sister generally acts as a go-between between him and her husband and tests her husband's reaction to the proposed match before her brother formally approaches him, thus saving her brother from the humiliation of rejection if her husband is strongly opposed to the match. She is prepared to work hard to prepare the ground for the smooth conduct of the formal marriage negotiations, as the marriage of her daughter to her BS is very likely also her own strong preference.

A boy's mother who is a sister of his prospective bride's father also usually acts as a go-between in negotiating the marriage of her son to her BD. As I mentioned before, the MBD–FZS marriage is usually desired by the girl's father. If that is so, he will let the boy's father know through his wife; and if the boy's father agrees to the marriage, he suggests it formally to his brother-in-law, knowing beforehand that he will not be rejected. It is of course possible that a man will want to arrange the marriage of his son to his matrilateral cross-cousin without the girl's father ever having hinted at it. In such a case the marriage will quite certainly also be the boy's mother's strong preference, and she will again act as a go-between between her husband and her brother. Her husband will learn through her what her brother's opinion is, and he can decide accordingly whether or not to enter into formal negotiations with him.

Through the informal sounding and mediation of either his sister or his wife the boy's father is saved from making proposals which would certainly be rejected; but cross-cousin marriages still have their risks for the men who try to arrange them, particularly if the girl has agnatic cousins of marriageable age. If a girl is asked for in marriage, it is her father's duty to inform his own brothers and to give them the option of claiming her for one of their sons. The girl's father can do this after his wife or sister has told him that the girl's cross-cousin would like to marry her; he does not have to wait for a formal proposal from the boy's father. He will, however, have to reveal the suitor's identity; and should the girl's agnatic cousin claim her, the cross-cousin's bid will be rejected even if it has not been made formally.

Most difficult to arrange are marriages between matrilateral parallel cousins. A woman can informally arrange with her sister the marriage of their children, but her manipulative power is in this case more limited than when she tries to arrange a marriage between her child and her brother's. The case is different in that it is not her own sibling but her sister's husband who has the ultimate authority over the prospective spouse of her child; and if he is as reluctant to arrange this particular marriage as her own husband may be, there is precious little that the sisters can do. A man is most reluctant to negotiate a marriage of his child to that of his wife's sister if another marriageable relative is at hand, because he has to negotiate it with his WZH, who in many cases is a complete stranger to him. If no kinship relationship exists between the two men, the social distance between them is so great and the mediating links so tortuous that most men do not consider these marriages to be any easier to negotiate than those between strangers.

The Berti disregard the plurality of possible connections between spouses when discussing the process of marriage negotiations in general terms; but in practice, when they exist, such connections are always utilised to facilitate the negotiations. Thus arrangements of marriages between cross-cousins or matrilateral parallel cousins are much easier than described above if the prospective spouses' fathers are, as is often the case, agnatic cousins. This, however, does not invalidate the accuracy of the Berti's general observation of the relative difficulty of arranging marriages between different categories of cousins, as outlined above. In practice, the marriage between patrilateral parallel cousins is still the easiest to arrange, as the negotiations involve men more closely related in kinship than in any other case.

Contexts of marriage preferences

For the Berti, the assertion that marriages between kin are better than marriages with strangers has several possible interpretations which can be held without commitment to any particular one. In this respect, it is not so much a proposition as what Sperber calls 'conceptual representation' (1982: 167–9). It has not a fully fixed propositional content but can be given different propositional interpretations by specifying the conceptual content of its elements. Such content may vary for different people, depending on their own experience, and it is certainly different for men and women. As the foregoing analytical description has shown, the propositional interpretations of the assertion are expressed by the Berti in terms of the pragmatic reasons for which certain marriages are better than others. These reasons themselves are formulated by considering specific marriage choices in the multiplicity of systemic contexts: the context of the relations between spouses, the context of economic and political relations and the context of the culturally-defined pattern of marriage negotiations. At the same time, the specific marriage choices are evaluated both in the context of asserted norms of kinship relations and in the context of the practice of these relations.

The question as to what reasons the Berti have for asserting that certain marriages are better than others cannot thus be answered by specifying one pragmatic reason for their marriage preferences. Different reasons are put forward for the same marriage preferences because different people consider each marriage in specific contexts selected from the multiplicity of contexts in which the desirability of any marriage can be evaluated. The different scales of preference expressed by men and women, for example, are the product of the different roles and social positions of men and women, whereby they see different contexts as relevant and consider different pragmatic reasons as important for their particular preferences. To concentrate the analysis on locating the reasons for the expressed preferences in only one of the contexts from which these preferences derive their meaning for the actors themselves would inevitably rob them of the multiplicity of their cultural meanings.

Interestingly enough, the analytical strategy of explaining the preference for FBD marriages in the Middle East has typically been aimed at defining one single specific context within which such a preference is meaningful. In most existing analyses (a notable exception being that of Bourdieu), the asserted preference is removed from the multiplicity of contexts in which it is obviously evaluated by the actors themselves and in which it can be understood as making sense. Equally interestingly, although the multi-contextuality of the preference is not acknowledged in the formulation of reasons for its existence, it is tacitly acknowledged in the refutation of specific explanations. Such refutations are typically based on privileging some specific context from the multiplicity of contexts in which the preference can be seen as meaningful.

The effort to preserve the property of the family has often been explicitly mentioned by the actors themselves as their motivation for marriages between patrilateral parallel cousins, and it has been used as an explanation for the preference for this type of marriage by a number of analysts (Granqvist 1931: 76–9; Chatila 1934; Rosenfeld 1957: 37; 1958: 1138; Peters 1963: 188; Baer 1964: 65–6); others have resorted to this explanation with certain qualifications (Goody 1983: 32, 43, 59; Tillion 1983: 105, 115). However, it has been rejected as implausible by Barth (1954: 170), who points out that FBD marriage would achieve its envisaged effect only if the norms of Koranic inheritance – according to which a daughter is given half of the amount received by a son – were strictly followed,[3] which very frequently is not the case.[4] He thus invokes the context of practice to invalidate the significance given to the FBD marriage in the context of asserted norms. He himself ascribes more importance to the context of the actual practice of power relations and suggests that, in view of the fact that the relationship between brothers represents the first potential line of fission between agnates, the significance of FBD marriage lies in the fact that, through it, 'the father receives political allegiance in his lifetime from his brother's son in return for the daughter which he gives him' (Barth 1953: 28, 69–70; 1954: 168). This argument has been criticised in turn by Murphy and Kasdan, who invoke the context of asserted norms to invalidate it, and point out that it is difficult to accept

Barth's explanation of the political strategies motivating FBD marriage in view of the fact that rather than a man giving his daughter to his BS, the BS has a normatively-asserted right to her (1959: 17–18).

The problem of formulating an adequate general theory of the asserted marriage preference thus hinges on the problem of defining the context from which the preference derives its significance. The explanations of the preference in terms of pragmatic reasons for which it is held or followed, whether they invoke the practical context or the normative one, are grounded in seeing the preference as instrumental in achieving particular goals; they differ merely in their view of what these goals are. In this respect, Barth's insistence on understanding the preference in the context of actually-existing interactions is obviously logically superior: if we assume that certain marriages are preferred because they offer distinct advantages to the actors, it is logical to assume that the actors evaluate these advantages on the basis of their knowledge of how social world is constituted rather than their notions of how it ought ideally to be constituted. The explanations which consider the preferences in the context of asserted norms see them also as instrumental in achieving practical goals. But by considering the expressed preferences in the normative context, they invariably make an unwarranted assumption of congruence between asserted norms and actual behaviour.

If we avoid the error of assuming such congruence and follow Barth's strategy, we are still faced with the problem of explaining why Barth's informants, who contract marriages between patrilateral parallel cousins because of political considerations, nevertheless assert that these marriages are preferable because they keep property in the family (Barth 1954: 167). Dismissing their asserted reasons as implausible is not an acceptable solution because it derives from the analyst's and not the actors' conception of contextual relevance; it substitutes the 'correct' reasons detected by the analyst for the 'false' reasons entertained by the actors (Stuchlik 1976). If we assume that the actors would not assert reasons for their marriage preferences which did not make any sense to them, our dismissal of them as implausible amounts to an admission that we have failed to see in what sense they could possibly be meaningful to the actors.

Considering the expressed marriage preferences as motivated by pragmatic reasons, Khuri suggests that the natives' statements to the effect that marriages between patrilateral parallel cousins maintain the property in the family need not be understood solely in the context of the Koranic norms of inheritance. He points out that property can be alienated not only by daughters but also by sons, through the payment of bridewealth (1970: 600). If a man marries a stranger, part of the property is alienated through the transfer of bridewealth. As only reduced bridewealth is usually transferred in the case of FBD marriages, the question of property alienation does not arise. But even if full bridewealth is transferred, no property is alienated if the man marries within the family. By the same logic it should be possible to argue that the transfer of dowry also does not alienate the family property in the case of FBD marriages. Although it is true that the Koranic laws of inheritance are often disregarded, the female property rights may be seen as recognised through dowry, which occurs widely in the Middle Eastern cultural area and which has been interpreted as a form of pre-mortem inheritance (Tambiah 1973: 64) or diverging devolution (Goody 1973: 17; 1976: 1983: 21).[5]

Although the cultural logic of the actors' property argument may become less problematic if this argument is considered in a context other than that of the Koranic laws of inheritance, I would suggest that it can be fully grasped only when the preferential marriages are seen not only as instrumental but also as expressive acts. I shall pick up this point again later.

For the moment I want to pay attention to other problems of the strategy which aims to explain the existence of a preference for FBD marriage in terms of pragmatic reasons motivating the actors' practice of such marriages. One such explanation sees this preference as an outcome of the effort to preserve family property. Another one, formulated by Khuri (1970), sees it is an outcome of the effort to facilitate the wife's adjustment to new relationships created through her marriage. Both explanations thus see the reasons for marriages between patrilateral parallel cousins in the advantages which accrue to the married couple themselves or to their offspring. But given that the marriages are, as a rule, arranged by the fathers or guardians, it is difficult to accept such advantages at face value as real motivations rather than legitimisations hiding the real motives of those who arrange the marriage.

This point can again be illustrated by considering the observable pattern of Berti marriages in the light of the explicit reasons which the Berti state for their preference of marriages between close kin. Their statements indicate that they are consciously motivated in their choice of spouse by specific strategic considerations. If that is so, the actual pattern of their marriages can be seen as the outcome of these conscious motivations. However, to be able to treat it as such, we have to be in a position to say that the reasons explicitly stated were the reasons actually motivating a specific choice and not merely rationalisations or legitimisations of a choice which was in fact motivated by completely different considerations. Any decision of this kind is further complicated by the fact that the same action (e.g. FBD marriage) could, in different cases, have been motivated by different considerations; while two different actions (e.g. marriage with a relative in one case and a locally endogamous marriage with an unrelated woman in another case) could have been motivated by the same considerations. When discussing specific marriages, I was able to elicit from the informants their specific reasons for them. However, at the level of these individual decisions, it is not possible to identify the reasons which have actually motivated the actors and to distinguish them from possible rationalisations, justifications and legitimisations. Other informants, when asked for their opinion about the veracity of these stated reasons, were not certain themselves.

It is, however, possible to be more certain when we move from the motivation of individual actors in specific concrete cases to categories of expressed reasons. When considering the two main categories of reasons for marriages between close kin, we are in a position to ascertain at least whether it is more likely that such marriages are contracted because they are seen as being of advantage primarily to the married couple themselves or to those who arrange them.

The first marriages of his children are always arranged by their father, if he is still alive. This does not necessarily imply that, when arranging them, the father will be primarily motivated by seeking specific advantages to himself alone, or to himself and his wife. The possibility cannot be excluded that he has, first of all, the future well-being of his children at heart, and that he will try to arrange marriages for them which are to their best advantage. It is possible that he will marry his children to their kin for the sole reason that such marriages have a better chance of enduring and of being less ridden with strains and conflicts than marriages to non-kin. If the desire for a stable marriage is the prime consideration guiding the choice of a spouse, we can assume that it will motivate not only the father who is arranging the marriage of his children, but also a man who is marrying for the second time, who pays his own bridewealth and who is free to choose his wife without interference from his father, as well as a man whose father is dead and who, in consequence, has a freer hand to choose his own wife than his counterpart whose father is still alive. If, as the Berti often say, it is the marriage with a kinswoman which is likely to endure and to be free of strains and conflicts, we may expect that the number of men who have themselves chosen kinswomen as their wives will be approximately the same as the number of men who have had them chosen by their fathers. Exactly the opposite is, however, empirically true. Out of 277 first marriages, only 84 (30.3 per cent) were between couples unable to trace any genealogical relations between them, whereas 193 (69.7 per cent) were between men and women genealogically related. Furthermore, of the 84 marriages between couples unable to trace any genealogical relationship, 64 (76.2 per cent) were marriages between members of the same maximal lineage, i.e. between members of the category of people who are presumed to be *ahal* in spite of the fact that an exact genealogical relationship between them is not known. On the other hand, out of 85 men marrying their second or third wife, 70 (82.4 per cent) married a woman to whom they were not able to trace any genealogical connection, whereas only 15 (17.6 per cent) married a kinswoman. Furthermore, of 70 marriages between couples unable to trace any genealogical relationship, only 10 (14.3 per cent) were marriages between members of the same maximal lineage.

When collecting census data in the field, I realised too late the significance of the fact of whether a man's father was dead or alive at the time of his first marriage, and I have this information for only 85 men in my census. Out of 59 men who married when their father was alive, 46 (78.0 per cent) married a kinswoman and only 13 (22.0 per cent) a woman to whom they could not trace a genealogical relation. Out of 26 men who married after the death of their father, only 12 (46.2 per cent) married a kinswoman, while 14 (53.8 per cent) married a non-relative. These figures not only confirm the father's decisive role in choosing his son's wife from among his kinswomen; they also indicate that a marriage with a kinswoman has to be seen as being primarily motivated by the advantages which accrue from it to the bridegroom's father or parents, rather than to the married couple themselves, and that the marriage pattern has to be seen primarily as the outcome of the strategic considerations of the parents and close relatives of the married couple (cf. Geertz 1979: 373–4; Maher 1974: 157; Youssef 1978: 80; Pastner 1981: 306, 316, n. 4).

Pragmatic reasons for marriage preferences

This last point impinges on some of the more general problems of explaining the preference for marriages between parallel cousins in terms of their pragmatic functions. I have tried to show that analysts who follow this strategy have elevated certain culturally-specific pragmatic reasons to the level of universal theory, and that the suggested refutations of such a theory were based on showing that these specific pragmatic reasons are inapplicable in specific cases. All this was possible because the search for a general theory of the existence of the preference in terms of pragmatic reasons is basically a search for an illusion.

My discussion of the reasons which the Berti give for their marriage preferences has indicated that a number of such reasons are recognised within one specific culture. Studies which pay attention to the pragmatic reasons expressly formulated by the actors are rare; as we have seen, if any attention has been paid to them at all, they were mostly declared as erroneous. A few studies in which the actors' reasons have been recorded confirm that different members of the same group or society consider marriages between cousins desirable for different pragmatic reasons, depending on their personal circumstances, ambitions and strategies

(Khuri 1970; Bourdieu 1977; Rosen 1984: 83). Where only one pragmatic reason has been specified for the existing marriage preference, we may assume that it is the one which, of the various reasons mentioned by the actors, makes most sense to the analyst.

If the existing literature on preferential FBD marriage is seen in this light, it clearly indicates that pragmatic reasons for the expressed marriage preferences vary from society to society as well as within particular societies. In view of this fact, it seems futile to see the reasons for the existence of FBD marriage in its practical utility. As Meeker expressed it, the marriage choice is 'not analyzable in terms of motivation and reason, but in terms of meaning of another kind' (1976: 394). It does not follow from this, however, that all analyses which concentrate on pragmatic reasons for this type of marriage are futile or useless, as has sometimes been summarily assumed. But it has to be realised what they can and what they cannot explain.

If what is to be accounted for is the observable marriage pattern, analytical attention has to be paid to actors' pragmatic reasons for preferring marriages between kin to those between strangers. This pattern is the result of a process of decision-making in which the different people involved have different degrees of freedom to follow their strategies and realise their goals.

As the previous discussion should have indicated, the strategic considerations of the parents and the culturally-constituted process of marriage negotiations complement and reinforce one another in generating the observable pattern of Berti marriages. Both processes are underpinned by the unequal roles of men and women, both in the domestic domain in which the strategic choices are made and in the public domain in which they are pursued. The husband's authority over his wife enables him to pursue his own strategies more easily and openly than she can her own; and the father's unequal authority over male and female children enables a son to influence the choice of his own spouse much more than a daughter can influence the choice of hers.

The actors' goals are of course neither totally idiosyncratic nor arbitrary; they are culturally defined, as are the acceptable strategies. In the course of their strategic behaviour, people thus resort to particular solutions because they exist as acceptable possibilities in the cultural framework within which the practical problems are solved. The preference for FBD marriage is such a cultural solution or resource, on which people can draw in their efforts to solve the various practical problems which face them. The observable marriage pattern is thus a result both of the people's marriage strategies and of the culturally-available options which constrain and canalise them. It can be accounted for only by taking into consideration both the personal goals and the culturally-determined strategies through which they are pursued. However when the problem to be explained is the form of the marriage pattern, what has to be realised is that it is not the asserted preference which is treated as problematic. When explaining the marriage pattern, it is possible to treat the existing preference as given, and to show how the actors can and do use it to solve various practical problems.

When, on the other hand, it is the preference which is treated as problematic and its existence becomes an object of explanation, it is the marriage pattern which has to be treated as given. It is hence wrong to assume that the strategic considerations which generate the pattern can account for its existence, as if the preference were an expression at the ideological level of the statistically prevalent practice.[6]

When explaining the marriage pattern, as I have said, it is possible to show how the actors use the existing preference to solve practical problems; however, it is not possible to argue conversely that it is these practical problems which generate the preference, i.e. that people have certain preferences because they serve useful practical functions. Such an argument, guided by the assumption that the asserted preference – like the observable marriage pattern – is the outcome of the actors' practical considerations, inevitably falls into the old fallacy of trying to explain the particular by reference to the general. The practical concerns of securing provision for old age, of rallying political support, of coping with emotional adjustment to family relations, or whatever, are universal concerns existing not only in societies which solve them through preferential FBD marriages. In other societies they are solved through other means. It is therefore impossible to argue that it is the practical problems which generate the preference for FBD marriages. No doubt, the preference is kept in existence by being perpetually revalidated in action; equally, no doubt, it would disappear from the cultural repertoire if that were not so. But to accept that it is the practical utility of the preference (or any other cultural notion for that matter) which prepetually revalidates it, and thus keeps it in existence, is not to accept that it was this practical utility which generated it in the first place.

As any pragmatic action logically presupposes the cultural notions which endow it with meaning (and as such constitute it as an *action*), the very presupposition of the meaningfulness of human actions would seem to lead to the inevitable conceptualisation of notions as ontologically prior to actions. The final result is the conceptualisation of culture as autonomous, ungoverned by practical reasons (Sahlins 1976). Such a conceptualisation has been the outcome of the realisation that it is not the practical utility of existing cultural notions which accounts for their existence; paradoxically, however, it has not itself overcome the difficulty which 'practical determinism' has faced when trying to explain the reasons for the existence of cultural notions. 'Cultural determinism', grounded in its conception of culture as autonomous, cannot explain them either; viewed in this light, they remain basically arbitrary, and have to be treated as given.

But to my mind, this impasse is not real. It seems real only as long as we consider the relationship between social structure and culture 'in bits', as Ortner and Whitehead have characterised it, 'nailing each [cultural] bit to some specific feature of social organization' (1981: 4). The difficulties of connecting these bits with one another persist, irrespective of whether the social-structural elements are seen as determining the cultural notions, or the cultural notions are seen as determining the social-structural arrangements, or the relationship between them is perceived as dialectical. Whatever the conceptualisation of the relations between social structure and culture, the failure to account for the existence of specific cultural notions derives ultimately from the failure to realise that culture itself has the properties of the system.

When trying to account for the existence of the preference for FBD marriage in the Middle East, we have to realise that, as a cultural notion, it exists independently of the practical function it might fulfil in the course of the strategic behaviour. As a cultural notion, it is related not only to the practical actions (in that it is kept in existence by being perpetually revalidated in action, and contributes to the patterning of the action through constraining or canalising actors' choices), but also to other aspects of the culture which at the same time defines the goals of the actions and the acceptable strategies for achieving them. Treating it, on analysis, as something related solely to the pattern of social action cannot adequately explain its existence.

We can now understand fully why parallel cousin marriage has been deemed sociologically inexplicable. It was precisely the consideration of the preference for this type of marriage solely in terms of its practical functions which led to this conclusion. The conclusion was then a logical consequence of the realisation that FBD marriage can serve widely different pragmatic functions under different economic, political, social and cultural conditions, and of the consequent realisation that it is futile to try to explain it by formulating one universal function which it invariably serves in all societies.

But the explanation can be achieved if the preference is considered not only in the context of social action but also in the context of other notions which constitute the culture of which the preference is a part, or when the preference is not merely considered as an instrumental device for achieving particular goals, but when attention is also paid to its expressive aspects. These are, of course, relevant to all the various contexts of social action within which the preference can be seen as functional. In other words, the preference can be explained when it is considered in the multiplicity of contexts in which the actors themselves consider it. It then becomes clear that FBD marriage is not only used by the actors to manipulate social relations to their advantage but that, at the same time, it expresses the very social relations which the actors try to manipulate through it.

In his discussion of the manipulation of patrilateral parallel cousin marriage, Bourdieu asks whether such marriage 'should be seen as the ideal, hardly ever achieved in practice, of accomplished marriage; or as an ethical norm (a duty of honour) which bears on every marriageable person but which can conceivably be broken (when circumstances make it impossible); or simply as a "move" recommended in certain situations. It is because it is all these things at once that it is a favoured object of manipulation' (Bourdieu 1977: 43). It is also because it is all these things that it is seen by the actors themselves as a preferable marriage.

Notes to Chapter 2

1 Similar sentiments are expressed by the Awlad 'Ali Bedouin of Egypt (Abu-Lughod 1986: 57–8).
2 The point that mothers and fathers can have different motivations in arranging their children's marriages has for the most part not been systematically examined in the literature on marriage negotiations in the Middle East. Pastner's study of the negotiation of marriages among the Zikri Baluch of Pakistan (1981) is a notable exception in this respect. See also Anderson 1982: 14.
3 Cf. also Khuri 1970: 598–600; Hilal 1972: 75–9; Guichard 1977: 34.
4 Agnatic marriages are more numerous among the marabout families in Kabylia than among the rest of the population (Bourdieu 1977: 204, n. 54). The ratio of internal marriages is thus higher among the pious. Could it not be that the pious, because they practise close kin marriages, can adhere to Koranic injunctions about inheritance without jeopardising their economic interests?
5 Murphy and Kasdan point out that the property argument ignores in any event 'the fact that the daughter of another family could well bring into the husband's group a most welcome inheritance, and we are thus able to use the same motivation to show that exogamy is a potential means of enhancing familial fortunes' (1959: 17). They raise the same point as the Moroccans who oppose FBD marriage: these point out that an in-marrying girl might bring new property with her (Geertz 1979: 373). The argument would of course hold only if the chances of preserving or enhancing familial fortunes through in-marriage and out-marriage were equal. As the wealth of different groups varies widely, exogamous marriage would enhance the group's wealth only if the bride came from a wealthier group than the husband, i.e. if a hypogamous marriage were the norm. But preference for hypergamy rather than hypogamy is another widely-expressed ideal throughout the Middle East. I shall return to the relation between the preference for close agnatic marriage and the preference for hypergamy (Chapter 5).

6 I suspect it was the fact that marriages with the FBD are merely preferred and not prescribed in the Middle East which lay at the root of this fallacy, which is underpinned by the assumption that – since we are dealing only with *preferences* – statistics are important, and that the statistical analysis of the marriage pattern can somehow throw light on the problem of the existence of the preference.

Chapter 3

The right to the FBD and the expressive aspect of patrilateral parallel cousin marriage

Marriage not only fulfils various pragmatic functions; it is also a culturally meaningful act. This chapter is concerned with this latter aspect; I shall argue that the potential of close agnatic marriages lies not merely in their specific pragmatic functions but also in their symbolic significance, and that they derive their meaning for the actors from both their pragmatic and their symbolic utility.

FBD marriage and the duty of honour

Under certain circumstances, the exercise of a man's right to marry a kinswoman becomes virtually expected; what is commonly conceptualised as a right comes to be seen as a duty.[1] The Berti ethnography again provides a convenient starting-point for the discussion of this aspect of patrilateral parallel cousin marriage.

Berti

Although it is the mother's and not the father's duty to control the daughter's conduct, the daughter's chastity is ultimately her father's responsibility. It is, first of all, his shame if his unmarried daughter becomes pregnant, for he should have been aware that women are irresponsible, or, as the Berti say, *awīn mā lēhum gharat kabīr* ('women do not care much'). He should have arranged for her to be married when she became a woman. On the other hand, he could not have done it if nobody asked for her in marriage, for, as the Berti say, 'you can take an animal to the market; you cannot offer your daughter to other people to marry her'. The shame hence does not befall the girl's father alone, but her kinsmen as well, for they should have married her if nobody else would and 'shrouded' (*satar*) her to protect themselves and her from shame. Under these circumstances, a man who marries an unrelated woman instead of a kinswoman has not simply refrained from exercising his right; he is failing in his duty, for he is helping her kin to avoid shame and not his own, as he ideally should. The saying *al mā ghatta gadahu, wala baghati gadahat al akhari* ('he who does not cover his own porridge bowl will not cover the bowls of others') conveys this message: he is a bad man, not conscious of his kinship responsibilities, and he will fail the expectations of others as he has failed the expectations of his kinsmen.

Although the Berti state that both the right and the duty to marry a kinswoman apply to all her kinsmen (*ahal*), these do not apply equally to all of them but are again graded like other rights and obligations in terms of kinship distance: the closer the kinship connection, the stronger both the right and the duty which it entails. The strongest responsibility for a woman's chastity befalls her father and brother, followed by the father's brother, the father's brother's son, mother's brother, mother's brother's son, etc. They exercise this responsibility by seeing to it that she gets married or by actually marrying her. What amounts, under certain circumstances, to an obligation to marry a kinswoman is thus directly related to the responsibility for her chastity.

For the Berti, patrilateral parallel cousin marriage is, on the one hand, just one of the possible marriages between kin. On the other hand, it is significantly different from any other kin marriage in that FBS is the only man whose right to marry his cousin is recognised as such and, at the same time, the only man who is seen as being in a certain respect obliged to marry her. The clear expression of the FBS's right is the custom whereby the father of a girl who has been asked for in marriage is obliged to inform those brothers of his who have marriageable sons, and to seek their approval of the proposed marriage. In fact, he should not consent to the marriage of his daughter without consulting his brothers.

When the father of a girl who has been asked for in marriage fulfils his obligation, informing his brothers and seeking their approval of the proposed marriage, he gives each one of them the opportunity to exercise the marriage right of his son and to claim the girl for him. When his daughter has not been asked for in marriage by anyone, and he likewise informs the brother who has a marriageable son of this fact, he makes an appeal to him to recognise his and his sons's responsibility. This is generally considered to be the only situation where it is appropriate for the girl's father to propose her marriage, in all other situations, it is up to the boy's father to make the proposal, and it is not considered appropriate for the girl's father to initiate marriage negotiations.

This does not mean that a man informs only his brothers when his daughter has been asked for in marriage, or that the never himself proposes his daughter's marriage except in the above-mentioned circumstances. If he is interested in marrying off his daughter to some kinsman other than his BS, he will hint to the prospective groom's father that her marriage to another man has been mooted; or he can even approach him if no such suggestion has been made. If he is conscious of propriety, he can always manipulate the situation in such a way that he will be formally approached by the father of the boy to whom he wants to give his daughter in marriage. But to inform kinsmen other than brothers is not normatively stipulated, whereas brothers always have to be informed. Even when a man himself wants to marry off his daughter to somebody other than his BS, he still has to inform his brothers if they have marriageable sons. If one of them does not agree with the proposed marriage, and suggests that the girl should marry his own son instead, her father's strategy can be effectively frustrated.

The fact that a man has to go through the motion of formally offering his daughter to his BS, irrespective of whom he himself would like to see as her husband, may in itself account for the statistical preponderance of patrilateral parallel cousin marriages. The cultural rules are formulated in such a way that any other marriage can take place only if both fathers desire it; patrilateral parallel cousin marriage, on the other hand, can take place when only the boy's father desires it. This, in itself, accords it a better probability ratio than any other form of marriage (see Bates 1974: 271 for the same point).

For the Berti, the preference for marriages between kin to those between strangers, or for marriages between patrilateral parallel cousins to those between other cousins, derives its meaning from the consideration of their economic and political advantages for the couple's parents and from the importance attached to the ease with which they can be negotiated and arranged. At the same time, these advantages derive from the consideration of marriages between kin in the context of ideals, rules and prescriptions pertaining to behaviour between kinsmen, as well as in the context of the actual interaction between them, which may differ considerably from its asserted normative ideal. Thus, from the point of view of the practical concerns of her father, a woman's marriage to her FBS may be seen as a better one when considered in the context of the norms of kinship relations; her marriage to her FZS may, however, be seen as a better one by her father when considered in the context of actual interaction between close agnates, which, as every Berti knows, often falls short of its asserted ideals.

The preference for marriages between close kin also derives its meaning from its instrumental utility for maintaining the man's honour, which is threatened by the irresponsible conduct of women. It was possible to discuss the practical advantages of particular marriages from the point of view of their unequal benefits for different individuals. Although fully aware of this inequality, the Berti strongly insist that marriages between kinsmen are good for everyone. The meaning of this insistence becomes obvious when such marriages are considered from the point of view of their role in maintaining the man's honour: a man who, through his marriage to a kinswoman, preserves the honour of his wife's kinsmen, also preserves his own.

As instrumental acts aimed at achieving specific economic and political goals, marriages derive their significance from the various contexts discussed in the previous chapter. As instrumental acts aimed at preserving kinsmen's honour, they derive their significance solely from the context of the ideals and norms of kinship behaviour. The rights of men to marry their kinswomen, interconnected with their responsibility for their chastity, themselves belong among the normatively-asserted rights and obligations of kinship.

In one sense, honour is a similar resource to property, economic cooperation or power. It too has to be secured and protected in the same way as all these other resources. On the other hand, if differs from them in that its norms cannot be manipulated, for the rules governing honour are only constitutive rules, not pragmatic rules. Even if economic cooperation or political support among kinsmen are normatively stipulated, in practice this normative obligation can be disregarded, for economic cooperation and political support can be obtained from strangers. Honour, however, exists only in so far as it is normatively asserted. It cannot be secured in any other than the normatively-prescribed way: unlike property, political power or economic cooperation, it cannot be secured by a contract with strangers; it can only be lost through such a contract.

The normative rules of kinship relations on which the notion of honour centres have a more general significance for the meaning of the asserted marriage preferences than the one which the concept of honour directly encompasses. This general significance can be grasped once it is realised that marriages between kinsmen are meaningful not only as instrumental but also as expressive acts. As instrumental acts they are aimed at achieving specific goals, whether these be economic cooperation, political support or honour. At the same time, they are also acts which express the asserted kinship solidarity. A man who marries off his daughter to a stranger without consulting a brother who has a marriageable son defies the norms of their relationship. By denying his daughter as his brother's daughter-in-law he clearly demonstrates a lack of concern for his brother's future. Equally, a man who allows his son to marry a stranger instead of his brother's daughter demonstrates a disregard for his brother's future as well as a lack of concern with his own and his brother's honour. The norms of their relationship are defied in this case in a way that could be matched only by their refusal to contribute to one another's *diya*. Both acts virtually amount to denying any bonds or kinship between them, and the Berti clearly see them as such. Not offering one's daughter formally in marriage to one's brother's son, like the refusal to contribute to one's brother's *diya*, is always a scandal which invites much comment, gossip and speculation. Just as marriages to strangers, when a marriageable kinswoman is available, express the denial of kinship solidarity, so marriage to a kinswoman is clearly seen as an expression of this solidarity. Apart from contributing to *diya* payments, marriage is the only act which has this symbolic significance.[2]

Agnatic solidarity and affinity

When the recognition of kinship ties, or the recognition of their significance, is symbolically asserted through marrying one's kin, what is being invoked is the normative context of kinship relations. In other words, it is the context of the asserted norms of kinship which makes a marriage meaningful as a symbolic pronouncement about the actual state of kinship relations. Without the invocation of the normative context no such meaning could be ascribed to or conveyed by the action. At the same time, every accomplished marriage to a kinswoman revalidates the norms of kinship solidarity of which it is itself an expression. It can be strategically exploited to achieve particular pragmatic goals because it has this significance for the maintenance of the asserted norms in the first place. Even if it is realistically recognised by the actors themselves that the asserted norms can be disregarded and violated in concrete actions, any sensible strategy can be designed only when the actions are considered as norm-governed. If they were seen only as subject to individual whim they would be unpredictable, and no sensible strategy could ever be formulated. The possibility of following particular strategies thus presupposes that the normative obligations which make the pattern of action predictable have perpetually to be acknowledged, confirmed and reasserted to be kept in existence. In this sense, the cultural domain impinges on the domain of actions through the mediating role of recognised norms (cf. D. M. Schneider 1976: 202–3). Marriages between kin play a crucial role in this dialectical relationship between the two domains: as they are themselves an expression of the recognition of the norms of kinship solidarity, each time they are contracted the validity of these norms is publicly acknowledged, confirmed and reasserted.

Solidarity and mutual support among agnates are normatively asserted throughout the Middle East. Even if their actual cooperation is undoubtedly often motivated by various pragmatic considerations, it still has to be justified in terms of the agnatic ideology which is normatively supposed to motivate it. Lancaster writes of the Rwala Bedouin that 'men can never co-operate with others from a different group without justification – friendship is not enough' (1981: 59).

In analysing the reasons for the observable cooperation between specific agnates or specific groups of agnates, most analysts have turned their attention to the pattern of marriage choices and to the resulting relations between men or groups of men through women. In his early paper on FBD marriage in Kurdistan, Barth pointed out that in the Middle Eastern social systems, where lineage exogamy is not prescribed, marriage patterns obviously do not function to define the relations between lineages. However, marriage relations and maternal ties still have 'relevance of a structural or specifically political nature' (1954: 165), and it is basically the political interests of the actors which determine their marriage choices. A man can rely on his brother's son's political support when he has married off his daughter to him without bridewealth (ibid.: 171). As Barth argued later, FBD marriage is the choice when opposed interests emerge between close collaterals, and the marriage becomes instrumental in either closing the rift or gaining the support of other collaterals in the face of the rift (Barth 1973: 13–14).[3] Barth also recognises that it is necessary to establish new alliances and renew old ones, for example with matrilaterals. This strategy is presumably accomplished through contracting marriages other than those with the FBD (1973: 14).

The merit of Barth's analysis is twofold: firstly, it is formulated in terms of actors' conscious motivations; secondly, it realises that any explanation of FBD marriage would be inadequate if it did not, at the same time, account for other types of marriage which occur concurrently with those between patrilateral parallel cousins. Yet his original argument that the FB is willing to forgo the brideprice in the case of his BS, because he can thereby rely upon his BS's complete political support, is difficult to reconcile with the fact that, generally, it is not the FB who gives his daughter to his BS but rather the BS who has a right to his FBD, whatever the girl's father's sentiments and motivations may be (cf. Patai 1955; 1962: 145 ff.). Barth himself mentions cases of violence resulting from the girl's father's disregarding his brother's son's right to the girl (1953: 26; 1954: 167). This would clearly indicate that patrilateral parallel cousin marriage is not only in the interest of the girl's father (Kressel 1986) but also in the interest of the girl's paternal cousin himself, or possibly that of his father, who has the responsibility for arranging his marriage. It seems that it is not so much the girl's father creating 'an obligation on the part of his brother's son to give him political support' (Barth 1954: 168), as rather the brother's son offering his support to his father's brother in exchange for the latter's daughter and thus preventing the rift along the first potential line of cleavage between collateral branches.

This may be a minor point. More important is the questionable validity of the more general assumption underlying Barth's analysis, which also underlies the analyses of those who stress the role of affinity and matrilateral kinship in generating solidarity among groups of men related through ties of agnatic kinship. This assumption derives from the notion of marriage as exchange. A gives a woman to B; B is in debt to A, a debt which is only partly offset by the payment of bridewealth; B's indebtedness is, of course, even more pronounced if no bridewealth or only reduced bridewealth is transferred, as is the case in FBD marriages (*pace* Cole 1984: 179–80), and he pays off the debt by lending his political support to A. It is a kind of exchange where women are exchanged not for other women but for political advantage (Lévi-Strauss, quoted in Pitt-Rivers 1977: 186, n. 86). Commenting on Barth's analysis, Khuri argues that 'it is very unlikely that a man would try to evoke loyalty among his nephews by marriage; they are already committed to support him in time of conflict' (1970: 601). Hilal (1972: 76) makes the same point. This argument is dubious, as it quite unjustifiably assumes that obligations will be fulfilled simply because they are normatively asserted; but the fact remains that mutual political support between FB and BS belongs among the normatively-asserted obligations between close agnates.

The fulfilment of obligations resulting from the debt relationship, or simply the expectation that the incurred debt will be repaid, is also normatively asserted. Of these two obligations, Barth clearly gives primacy to the latter. His analysis, like Schapera's analysis of Tswana marriages (1950, 1957, 1963), is thus based on the assumption that the normatively-stipulated obligations underlying contractually-established relationships (affinity) have a more binding force than normatively-stipulated obligations of kinship (agnation). The same assumption could be expressed by saying that it is not the normative obligations of agnation, but the normative obligations of affinity, which generate the desirable political support. Affinity, simply, surpasses agnation in creating the mutuality of interests (cf. Rosenfeld 1968: 251, 255).[4]

This assumption underlies, for example, Cole's analysis of affinal and matrilateral ties among the Āl Murrah Bedouin of the Empty Quarter of the Arabian peninsula.

Āl Murrah

In spite of the fact that Āl Murrah usually describe their social organisation 'exclusively in terms of patrilineal descent' (Cole 1984: 181; figures in parentheses in this section refer to pages in this text), Cole argues, for

Agnatic solidarity and affinity

example, that they make no special effort to cooperate in herding 'unless marriage ties exist' (180), and suggests that they are themselves aware that 'affinal ties sometimes override consideration of descent' (178). In his view, agnation is thus merely an ideological screen erected by the male sector of the population (177, 178), and it is affinal and matrilateral links that really determine concrete action.

To dismiss ideology in this way, as having no relation to observable action, may make the system more easily understandable to the anthropologist; but it also raises important questions, ones which remain unanswered. If agnatic ideology is so pervasive, in spite of the importance of the alliance through marriage and the factual bilaterality of the system, what is its function? Why do the actors delude themselves by explaining what they do by reference to it?

In the rest of this chapter I am going to suggest that the perceived discrepancy between 'ideology' and 'practice' is a mirage of our own making, and that the above questions are in fact misconceived. We have been led into posing them only by following too rigidly our preconceptions about what is 'basic' to the system we are trying to comprehend. In particular, I would argue that the postulated discrepancy between the native 'ideology' and the 'reality' as perceived by the anthropologist is a result of the anthropologist's interpretation of marriages as instrumental acts (cf. 172) and his disregard for their meaning as expressive and symbolic acts.

Although I do not wish to deny the importance of affinity in structuring the observable relations among Āl Murrah in many cases which Cole mentions, it seems to me that his insistence that affinal links between agnates matter more than their genealogical links is at least partly mistaken. When due attention is paid to marriages as symbolic or expressive acts, most of his evidence for the importance of affinity among agnates becomes rather dubious.

Thus, to give an instance, when 'households related through FBD marriage' camp together during the winter grazing (180), it does not necessarily mean, as Cole claims, that they do so because they are affines. As will be argued later in this chapter, they may come together because they are particularly close agnates, which is clearly suggested to the Āl Murrah by the fact that they are intermarried. Their actions are thus fully in line with the proclaimed ideals.

When men who visit members of minimal lineages other than their own are 'keen to find out who is married to whom', it does not necessarily mean that they try 'to understand the totality of one's social relationships'. They may in fact try to establish 'the patrilineal relationships of the people involved', which are *not* 'easily discerned by knowing the minimal lineage name of an individual' (179) given that 'the internal relationships of the lineages within the clan is [*sic*] of little importance to the Āl Murrah. Usually they are simply named without stating the relationships between them, and in most instances the exact relationships are unknown except to some old men, although everybody knows that some lineages are closer to some than to others' (176). If, as among the Rwala (cf. pp. 88–90 below), the occurrence of marriages between agnates is taken as a sign of their genealogical closeness, by inquiring into who is married to whom the men may in fact try to find out *which* lineages out of those they visit are close to their own. Their apparent interest in affinal relationships is not necessarily evidence that any importance is attached to affinity as such; affinity among agnates could be noted simply because it is an index of their genealogical closeness.[5]

FBD marriages, affinity and ties of matrilateral kinship

Another assumption underlying the analysis of the role of affinal links among agnates handles affinity slightly differently. It postulates that intermarriages among close agnates create links of affinity and matrilateral kinship, and that these links, which parallel the agnatic connections, contribute in a considerable way to strengthening the solidarity between the agnates concerned. As a result, the mutuality of their interests is fostered and their political integration enhanced. This assumption is therefore not based on a differential evaluation of agnation and affinity but rather on the mechanical adding up of these two components: the denser the network of mutual connections between agnates, the greater their solidarity.[6]

Marriages between close agnates obviously create a multiplicity of connections between them; but, as Peters rightly warns, 'unseen connections, obvious perhaps to the anthropologist, are irrelevant' (1976: 40). Whether it is postulated that the affinal connection surpasses the agnatic one in importance or merely that it adds an additional strength to it, the attribution of significance to affinal relationships among agnates is valid only in so far as it corresponds to the actors' own evaluation of their mutual ties. To test its validity, I turn to Cohen's analysis of the correlation between the increase of patrilateral parallel cousin marriages and the increase in the political significance of patronymic groups (*hamūla*) in Arab border villages in Israel. This analysis provides an ideal test case because it is quite explicity grounded in the assumption that agnatic solidarity is greater the denser the network of mutual connections between agnates. Moreover, Cohen's ethnography gives an indication of the actors' view and experience of agnatic and affinal links, which is impossible to glean from most other ethnographic descriptions of the marriage preferences, strategies and patterns in the Middle East.

Arab border villages in Israel

The Arab border villages in Israel are divided into a number of units called *hamūla*. The unity of hamula members is expressed in the idiom of patrilineal descent (Cohen 1965: 3, 107; figures in parentheses in this section refer to pages in this text), and consistent with this is the extension of agnatic kinship terms to all hamula members (107): thus, both in the conceptualisation of the relationship among its members and in its expression through kinship terminological usage, the hamula clearly constitutes a distinct group of agnates. The importance of agnatic descent as the ideologically-asserted principle of recruitment of hamula members is further indicated by the fact that members of a hamula who are not descended from one ancestor through historically valid patrilineal links always try to conceal this fact, and that it is considered derogatory to point to the mixed-descent origin of hamula members (109).

A hamula has a distinct corporate identity, the character of which has, however, changed considerably over time. During the Mandate Period, the strength of the hamula's corporate identity was severely eroded by the internal differentiation of its members in terms of wealth based on the ownership of land, and the dominant cleavage in the village followed class lines. The political importance which hamulas traditionally enjoyed was assumed instead by the larger armed nationalistic factions (8). After the establishment of the state of Israel, class differences were progressively eroded as the agricultural basis of the traditional economy declined and new economic opportunities opened for the villagers within the Israeli economy. This development was paralleled by the strengthening of the hamula's corporate identity, the main manifestation of which was the re-emergence of the hamula as the main political unit within the village: the dominant cleavage in the village started to follow hamula lines (9).

The strengthening of hamula loyalties and the renewed emphasis on agnatic ties (9) was accompanied by growing opposition to inter-hamula marriages (71–93) and by an increase of 7.6 per cent in the ratio of in-hamula marriages to total marriages (marriages with FBD increased by 3.4 per cent and marriages with other agnates within the hamula by 4.2 per cent) (93).

Every in-hamula marriage creates new ties of affinity among hamula members and, in the next generation, gives rise to ties of matrilateral kinship among them. Cohen puts a strong analytical emphasis on these ties as means of promoting greater solidarity within the group of agnates:

But the question remains whether the members, or the domestic groups, of a hamula are, in fact, linked together mainly by patriliny and by the values and beliefs associated with it. The sentiment aroused by the belief in being 'from one sinew' or in having 'the same blood', may well be an important link, though it is difficult to determine how important it is. However, associated with this sentiment are the more concrete links created by the web of affinal and matrilateral ties, by neighbourliness, and by close co-operation in economic and ceremonial activities.

If, for the sake of analysis, the link of political patriliny is ignored for the time being, the hamula will appear as a group of men who are mainly linked through their marriages to one another's daughters (110–11).

But even if hamulas are not totally endogamous, the substantial proportion of the internal marriages which each has links its members together intensely and, to some extent, marks the hamula off from other hamulas in this respect (112).

[Relationships created by marriages within the hamula] are most intense and complex because they overlap, and also cut across each other. The men are linked together in a variety of ways which impose on them different obligations towards each other. Through the recurrence of in-hamula marriages over a period of time, men who are related matrilaterally by one marriage also become affines by virtue of another marriage and so on (113).

... without political patriliny, the hamula consists of a number of domestic patronymic units, often living in the same village, which are intensively linked together by overlapping and cross-cutting matrilateral and affinal ties. This is equal to saying that the hamula is linked together, as a group, mainly through the women of the group (118).

Evidently, then, Cohen feels that the links created by the affinal and matrilateral ties among hamula members are more concrete than the agnatic ties – they link them together more intensely. There is a qualitative difference between affinity and agnation: the former is real and its binding force is unquestionable; the latter is merely ideologically asserted and its binding force is open to question. Hence, in analysis, the patrilineal links can be bracketed off. The underlying assumption is clearly formulated here. It is an assumption which its grounded in a rather mechanistic conception of social solidarity: solidarity is increased either by another link being added to the agnatic ties already existing among the group members, on the grounds that the greater the number of ties among group members, the greater is the group's solidarity; or it is increased through preventing agnatic and affinal connections of group members pulling in different directions, on the grounds that the less diverse the ties among group members, the greater again is their solidarity. Such an assumption arbitrarily ascribes a greater strength and concreteness to specific ties, and also assumes that the strength of each tie is automatic.

Cohen indicated the correlation between the revival of the hamula as a political unit and a stricter control exercised collectively by the hamula over the movement of its women in marriage (93, 121); and he has clearly stated that the 'the degree to which this control is effectively exercised, is, ultimately, an index of the political unity of the hamula' (121). I would suggest, however, that we gain a more accurate insight into this correlation between agnatic solidarity and in-hamula marriages if we abandon a mechanistic view of social solidarity. Instead, our analysis should be built on the more realistic assumption that any connection has an effect on the solidarity of hamula members only if its binding force is recognised as such, and utilised, by the actors themselves. We can estimate this strength by paying attention to the value which the actors ascribe to particular connections. The ethnographic evidence indicates that, as the emphasis on patriliny strengthened, the importance which the Arabs in Israel ascribed to matrilateral and affinal links cutting across hamula boundaries weakened considerably (9, 63 f., 92).

When Cohen insists, in spite of this fact, that the affinal links among hamula members contribute in a decisive way to their mutual solidarity, he is forced to ascribe a different effect on solidarity to affinal links between members of the same hamula than to those between members of different hamulas. However, there is no evidence in his writing that the actors themselves evaluate the strength of affinal links within the hamula differently from those existing across hamula boundaries. What seems to differ for the actors is not the strength of the bond between affines who are not agnates and between affines who are, but the strength of the bond between agnates (however additionally related) and affines and matrilaterals (who are not agnatically related).

If that is so, it is obviously incorrect to see the cause of increased agnatic solidarity in the increase of in-hamula marriages. In cause-and-effect terms, both the increase in in-hamula marriages and the decrease in affinal solidarity would have to be seen as effects of an increase in agnatic solidarity. I would argue, however, that even this view is inaccurate, and that the increases in agnatic solidarity and in-hamula marriages are not causally but logically related. I would argue, further, that it was the symbolic connotations of in-hamula marriages that linked such marriages logically to the emphasis on patriliny. In other words, the growing emphasis on patriliny and the accompanying emphasis on in-hamula marriages were not logically interrelated at the level of their consequences for the behaviour of hamula members but at the level of their symbolic meanings.

The villagers subscribe to the view that the ideal marriage is that between close agnates: certainly the right of a man to marry his patrilateral parallel cousin is normatively recognised (71, 72, 74–5, 121); and the order of a particular cousin's priority right to marriage is determined by his genealogical nearness to the woman, so that a first parallel cousin has priority over the second, etc. (121). The preference for marriages between close agnates thus gives meaning to these matches as symbolic expressions of the agnatic closeness of the spouses. If the right to marriage derives from close agnation, a man who presses his right to marriage defines his relationship with his prospective bride as one of close agnation. At the same time, the recognition of his marriage right by others amounts to a recognition of the premise on which the right is based. This means that any marriage right which has been recognised becomes a publicly-expressed acknowledgement of the close agnatic links between the spouses. The meaning of the match as a symbolic expression of such links derives from the basic syllogism: close agnates have a right to marry; A's right to marry B has been recognised; A and B are close agnates.

Marriage can, of course, be manipulated like any other symbol. When the emphasis on agnatic solidarity strengthens, it can be expected that marriages between agnates will be encouraged. The recognition of a man's right to marry a girl from his own hamula (90, 121, 123) is clearly a new phenomenon in Arab villages: the strong emphasis on the norm of marriage within the hamula has been increasingly laid down in recent years (93), when hamulas have become revitalised as the main political units and the struggle of each hamula for prestige and political power within the village has been accentuated. All this can be seen as a logical outcome of the conscious manipulation of the symbolic significance of agnatic marriages as visible manifestations of the recognition of the strength of agnatic connections. Even more significant in this context is the emergence of the notion that a man's marriage to a hamula girl is not only his right but his duty (80): just as a marriage within the hamula is a symbolic expression of the closeness of the agnatic connection between hamula members, a marriage to a stranger – when there is a marriageable girl within the hamula – can be construed as a denial of a close agnatic connection. As such, it undermines the agnatic ideology in terms of which the hamula's solidarity is formulated. The conflict which followed a man's attempt to marry a girl from a different hamula, against the wish of her own agnates to marry her off to one of their number (see 71–93), is a clear indication of people's sensitivity to the symbolic meanings of inter-hamula and in-hamula marriages.

An analysis which attributes the increased solidarity of the hamula to the creation of affinal links among its members misses the full significance of the cultural logic underlying the correlation between the political unity of the hamula and the increased control of the movement of women in marriage. It fails to grasp that both inter-hamula and in-hamula marriages are symbolically significant. By seeing the grounds for in-hamula marriages merely in creating the ties of affinity among hamula members, it has to postulate that marriages between direct patrilateral parallel cousins contribute less to hamula unity than those between more distant cousins (112), leaving unexplained why the increase in political unity has been accompanied by an increase in the ratio of marriages between both distant *and* direct cousins. If we see agnatic marriages as contributing to hamula unity by providing a means by which the members of the hamula can symbolically recognise the closeness of the agnatic ties, we obviate these difficulties.

FBD marriages and agnatic genealogy

When marriages among kin are proscribed, each marriage creates new ties of affinity which bind together the kinsmen of both spouses. When marriages among kin are preferred and consistently practised, the continuation of kinship ties which existed prior to the marriage inevitably affects the newly-created relations of affinity. Any analysis is bound to distort the meaning of both kinds of ties if it ascribes an importance to affinal ties which is at variance with the importance ascribed to them by the actors. There is ample evidence from all over the Middle East that, when people are related both consanguineally and affinally, affinity yields to consanguinity. The precedence given to consanguinity is signified by the fact that consanguineous kinship terms continue to be used by those who became affinally related, and are not replaced by affinal terms; and by the fact that the behaviour appropriate among them as kinsmen either continues unaltered, or significantly modifies behaviour which would be appropriate among them as affines (see, for example, Pastner 1981: 314).[7] Murphy and Kasdan have argued that 'parallel cousin marriage contributes to the extreme fission of agnatic lines in Arab society, and, through in-marriage, encysts the patrilineal segments. Under these circumstances, integration of larger social units is accomplished vertically, through genealogical reckoning to common ancestors, and not horizontally, through affinal bonds' (1959: 27). I suggest that agnation, and not mutual affinal ties among its members, is the source of integration even within the 'encysted' patrilineal segments. Patrilateral parallel cousin marriage and strong emphasis on agnation are logically linked in a dialectical relationship. If marriages between agnates are consistently practised over generations, paternal and maternal ascendants merge (Murphy and Kasdan 1959: 22; Barth 1973: 12). This may be not only an unforeseen consequence of the existing marriage strategies, but also their consciously-pursued goal (cf. Peters 1960: 44; 1965: 133; Barclay 1964: 118; Maher 1974: 158, 160). When connections are traced through agnatic lines wherever possible, all kinship is effectively reduced to agnation (cf. Pehrson 1966: 35). Even if such an extreme notion of kinship is far from general, the tendency to emphasise agnation above any other connection is widespread throughout the Middle East, at least in situations where corporate interests are concerned. I would suggest that it is the meaning ascribed to close agnatic marriages that upholds the strong agnatic ideology; it does so because it facilitates the tracing of connections almost exclusively through agnatic links. In a culture in which close agnatic connections predetermine the ideal marriage unions, every marriage between agnates becomes logically a signifier of their closeness. The more intermarriages occur between specific categories of agnates, the more visibly is their closeness symbolically demonstrated. The intermarriages between agnates thus bring them closer together, not through creating numerous ties of affinity and matrilateral kinship among them but through consistently signifying their agnatic closeness, which then becomes ultimately expressed through its own appropriate symbols. Again, this process may best be brought out by a concrete ethnography.

Bedouin of the Negev

The core of each sub-tribe of the Bedouin of the Negev, in southern Israel, is formed by a group of men who consider themselves agnatically descended from the tribe's ancestor. Around this core-group accrete other agnatic groups and individual families (Marx 1967: 65–6; figures in parentheses in this section refer to pages in this text). Each core-group is linked to one of the accreted groups and numerous intermarriages exist between these two allied groups, which engage in a limited political collaboration (174–5).

The Bedouin view the relationship between allied groups vaguely as one between agnates. The allied groups are spoken of as 'close' (*garīb*), closeness (*garābah*) being clearly associated with agnation. The intermarriages between members of the groups give rise to affinity and matrilateral kinship between them. But even if the nearest genealogical connection between the men of the two groups is traced through a woman, their relationship is seen as an agnatic one and they refer to one another by agnatic kinship terms (175–6).

Marx himself sees the notion of agnatic relationship between allied groups as a function of their political collaboration, which in itself has been made possible through their numerous intermarriages: political relationships among the Bedouin are always expressed in agnatic terms (175). Undoubtedly, if political collaboration is expected between agnates, wherever it occurs, it may connote the existence of agnatic relationship. This may account for the notion of 'closeness' between allied groups but fails to explain why 'one does not consider every member of the opposite group as an agnate, except those who are one's kin' (175). All members of the allied groups, and not only those linked through kinship ties, are presumably involved in political collaboration. Why then should the existence of an agnatic connection be expressed in the kinship terminological usage only in the case of the latter?

In stressing the role of intermarriages in forging the alliances, Marx does not take into account the fact that they occur in the context of an already-existing notion of closeness between the intermarrying groups, which derives from their assumed – though not precisely traceable – descent from the tribal ancestor (66, 71–2, 131, 133). The intermarriages between the groups are thus intermarriages between agnates. Once this is realised, the extension of agnatic kinship terminology to those related through ties of cognatic kinship starts to make sense. Marriage between close agnates is the cultural preference among the Bedouin; certainly the right of a man to marry his patrilateral parallel cousin is recognised (228). Against the background of this notion, which sees marriages between agnates as a prerogative of their closeness, any marriage between agnates may be construed as signifying their close connection: why should they have married unless they were close? Once a close agnatic connection is presumed to exist, it becomes legitimate to express it through the use of appropriate kinship terminology. In this process, the kinship terminological usage becomes only a codification of the relationships which the intermarriages construct.

In turn, the use of agnatic kinship terms among the related members of allied groups must have a profound effect on genealogies. In a situation where all members of a descent group are referred to and addressed by the same terms as close agnates (223), the use of agnatic kinship terminology must eventually be perceived as signifying membership of the descent group, and it seems almost inevitable that this in turn will be codified by a corresponding adjustment of the genealogy. A group which may have started its relations with a core-group of the sub-tribe by exploiting a vague notion of being descended from an ancestor who was 'perhaps a son of the tribe's founding ancestor and whose name was lost in the passage of time' (66), is likely to end up by tracing its descent from the tribal ancestor through the same genealogical links as the core-group itself, and thus fully to merge with it.

FBD marriages and the creation of agnatic ties

The same process of creating an agnatic relationship through marriage where previously no agnation has been genealogically demonstrated is mentioned by Aswad for the settlers on the Amik Plain in southern Turkey.[8] Distant relatives, and possibly even unrelated persons, come to be seen as agnates after the occurrence of an intermarriage which has been classified as a marriage between patrilateral parallel cousins (Aswad 1971: 84). The importance of ideologically-asserted agnatic solidarity – according to which, the closer the agnatic link the stronger the solidarity – is witnessed by the often-quoted saying: 'Me against my brother, me and my brother against my cousin, me and my brother and my cousin against the outsider'. Aswad points out that the actual alignments would be more accurately expressed by saying: 'Me against *some* of my brothers, me and *some* of my brothers against *some* of my cousins, me, *some* of my brothers and *some* of my cousins against *some* outsiders' (ibid.: 82). From a multiplicity of available agnatic connections, only some are thus seized upon in action. In spite of the selective process at work, the action can still be justified and made meaningful in terms of the all-pervasive and unqualified ideology. The process through which the veracity of the agnatic ideology is maintained, in spite of the pragmatic utilisation of the ties of affinity and bilateral kinship, and in spite of the fact that selection of *some* agnatic ties at the expense of others necessarily underlies the actual alignments, is again best illustrated by specific ethnography.

Rwala Bedouin

The Rwala clearly see the agnatic ideology as motivating all economic and political cooperation (Lancaster 1981: 59; the figures in parentheses in this section refer to pages in this text). 'Matrilateral relationships (and any others for that matter) are never organised in the same way that patrilineal ones are; they are simply used in an *ad hoc* manner' (41). At the same time, the occurrence of FBD marriages is clearly taken as a sign of the genealogical closeness of intermarrying groups; and such marriages are instrumental in manipulating the genealogy to express the actual relations among groups in terms of the agnatic ideology. Among the groups equidistant in terms of their agnatic genealogy, those linked together through FBD marriages are considered to be more closely related agnatically than those between whom such marriages do not take place, and this closeness is eventually expressed through the adjustment of genealogy. As it is known that the Rwala always marry their patrilateral parallel cousins, the presumed genealogical closeness or distance of specific groups can always be clinched by the statement: 'We must be more closely related because we inter-marry more frequently' (31–2); alternatively, it can be argued that specific groups are more distantly related as there are no intermarriages between them (34). 'The argument rests on the premise that marriage between close patrilateral parallel cousins is the norm, therefore frequent marriages between two groups means [*sic*], *ipso facto*, that they are closely related' in the male line (36). 'By the time the process [of intermarrying] has continued for a generation or two the more distant genealogical details are forgotten and the f.f.fs of the groupn will "become" brothers: there will be no one alive who can deny it with any authority and the facts of the marriage will prove it to be true' (36). Although, no doubt, the actual choice of marriage partners is motivated economically or politically, or guided by consideration of their reputation, in many cases the Rwala consciously and deliberately use their marriage strategies to manipulate genealogical relations in order to produce a desirable form (36 ff.).

We are clearly dealing here with a system in which agnatic ideology and close agnatic marriage are logically interrelated. Close agnatic marriages make it possible to maintain the agnatic ideology which is used to justify the economic and political cooperation, and which helps to explain the existing cooperation in terms of this ideology. Affinal links are not dismissed from consideration; they are noted, however, not because they are affinal relationships, but because they are indices of agnation.

Lancaster's analysis clearly shows that close agnatic marriages keep the changing realities of political and economic cooperation, themselves determined by practical considerations, in line with the enduring ideal:

... when faced with five groups of cousins, all equally related to you, how do you decide which ones to choose to cooperate with and which to discard? For you must co-operate to survive. Even if a purely pragmatic choice is made, it has to be justified in genealogical terms, so the genealogy has to be fudged to fit reality. The easiest way to do this is to change one existing relationship into another; a son becomes a brother or an uncle a father. This is fine provided your complementarily opposed segment, the groups you are shedding, don't contest it. So you have to have a private way of fudging the genealogy. This is only possible through women, for men and the patrilineal genealogy are very public indeed – they must be so that you can demostrate how you fit into the total system.

Preferred marriage within the patriline and especially at the level of f.f.b.d.d. fulfils all the conditions very nicely. You remember the necessary parts of the genealogy to fit yourself into the overall society, while at the same time you generate the lines of division that will later be used to justify the shedding of the subgroup. It is much easier for a son-in-law to become a son, for he must have been more closely related or he wouldn't have been a son-in-law in the first place. Equally, a subgroup to be excluded becomes more distant because you don't marry with them. They cannot complain that they are really close because they can never demonstrate it (50).

Among the Rwala, where marriages among distant agnates narrow down the genealogical distance among them in this way, and thus bring the relations of cooperation in line with the asserted agnatic ideology,

bilateral ties are certainly used but they never constitute an alternative organised system. The generative genealogy, although it may work bilaterally, in that men who are more closely related through women 'become' brothers or father and son, is never seen to do so. After all, the whole point of the generative geneaology is to make sense of pragmatic groups in strict patrilineal terms. When taxed with using bilateral relationships in this manner, men readily admit to it but only as an exception and anyway 'if they were not actually brothers, they must have been very closely related (patrilineally) or the relationship between them couldn't have existed' (42).

The expressive aspect of FBD marriage

The data on the Bedouin of Negev, the Rwala and the settlers on the Amik Plain, as well as other Middle Eastern societies (J. Schneider 1971: 19), clearly indicate that marriages between agnates not only are symbolic expressions of their closeness but also are, at the same time, instrumental in producing it: those who consider themselves only remotely related through assumed agnatic descent effectively become close agnates in consequence of their intermarriage. While agnatic ideology justifies, validates or legitimises the group's solidarity, it is the close agnatic marriages that are the most important expression of agnation. As among the Berti, marriages are clearly seen both as instrumental and as expressive acts.[9]

The expressive or symbolic aspect of close agnatic marriages is subject to the actors' strategic manipulation to no lesser degree than is their pragmatic function.[10] The ultimate effect of this manipulation is that the pragmatically determined solidarity is brought in line with the asserted ideology, in terms of which it can retrospectively be explained and made meaningful. However, of necessity, this point has had to remain rather speculative. As Lancaster pointed out, if the notion of agnation as determining the observable cooperation is to be sustained as valid, the fact that agnation itself is the product of strategic manipulation cannot be admitted (Lancaster 1981: 42). We are perpetually confronted with the product, while its production remains forever hidden. The main concern of the next chapter is to show further that this point is, nevertheless, a valid one. The strategic manipulation of the symbolic significance of close agnatic marriages is particularly apparent in situations where groups differing in status or power are specifically concerned with preserving or enhancing the prestige which they enjoy. To demonstrate further the role of this strategic manipulation in producing agnation, I pay specific attention to such situations in the next chapter.

Notes to Chapter 3

1 Most anthropologists, following the natives' generalisations, consider marriage to the patrilateral parallel cousin as constituting the man's right. Bourdieu rightly points out that a man's supposed right to his parallel cousin may in fact be a duty under certain circumstances (1977: 46–8); and marriage to their patrilateral parallel cousins may be pressed on sons by their fathers and

fathers' brothers, even if no right to marry an FBD is recognised (Anderson 1982: 14, 22).
2 The expressive aspect of *diya* payments is discussed in Holy 1974: 137–42.
3 Aswad's diachronic analysis of marriage patterns among settlers on the Amik Plain, in southern Turkey, supports Barth's conclusion by showing clearly that few marriages are contracted between the children of brothers competing for leadership of a strong patrilineal unit. The brothers competing for leadership arrange marriages of their children with the children of those brothers who do not oppose them, and with the children of their first patrilateral cousins (Aswad 1971: 75–99). Aswad's data support the interpretation of patrilateral parallel cousin marriages as indicators of existing agnatic closeness: as the notion of who is a close agnate (in the political sense) differs from time to time according to the state of competition for group leadership, so does the strategy of marriage.
4 The Comaroffs suggest that, apart from being grounded in an unjustified assumption of the determining effect of proclaimed norms on behaviour, another basic deficiency of this argument derives from disregarding the fact that an agnatic marriage 'often occurs within a field of individuals already connected by precisely the kinds of bonds which it is supposed to create'. They point out that, in consequence, 'we are *not* dealing simply with the normative transformations of social linkages' (Comaroff and Comaroff 1981: 36).
5 Cole mentions that the Āl Murrah use the terms *nasib* (denoting in-law) and *khal* (mother's brother) equally, whether they refer to close or distant agnates. This he takes to be 'symbolic of their recognition of affinity and matrilaterality, even among close agnates' (1984: 181). Elsewhere, however, he indicates that the term *ibn 'amm* (father's brother's son) is used in these instances (Cole 1975: 84); the latter terminological usage is in line with the practice of other Bedouin tribes.
6 Bourdieu's and Abu-Lughod's analyses represent notable exceptions to the view that ties of affinity among agnates contribute to their integration. Although Bourdieu clearly sees patrilateral parallel cousin marriage as strengthening the integration of the agnatic group (1977: 64–6), he interprets it as the 'most absolute affirmation of the refusal to recognize the relationship of affinity' (ibid.: 44). Abu-Lughod argues that patrilateral parallel cousin marriage 'is ideal because it follows the patrilineal principle, subsuming the marital bond under the prior and more legitimate bond of kinship' (1986: 145).
7 Shahsevan ethnography provides a negative case which supports my general argument. The crucial affinal relationship among them is that between brothers-in-law. It is characterised by close friendship and generalised reciprocity, which is expected to be permanent. In this respect, it contrasts with the relationship between patrilateral cousins, who compete over common resources. Tapper argues that the rarity of FBD marriages among the Shahsevan is 'in large measure due to a basic opposition between relations proper to brothers-in-law and those characteristically found between FBS's. Qualities characteristic of the relationship between brothers-in-law 'are much more easily found in relations between more distant agnates and other kinds of

kinsmen, among whom there are likely to be fewer of the common material interests (property, enforced cooperation), differences over which threaten the ideal of amity in the case of closer agnates' (R. Tapper 1979: 146).
8 It is also alluded to by Tillion, who suggests that in the Maghreb the past exchange of women is 'considered a presumption of kinship in the paternal line' (1983: 113).
9 For additional discussion of the symbolic aspect of FBD marriages see Bates 1974: 282; Christensen 1982; Kressel 1986.
10 For the analysis of marriage choices from this point of view see, for example, Ferdinand 1982.

Chapter 4

Agnation, power and the symbolic significance of FBD marriage

One cultural theme which seems to recur with astonishing regularity throughout the Middle East is that, whenever differences in status or power between groups are perceived or acknowledged to exist, they are legitimised by invoking the antiquity of the descent line of the more powerful group and the purity of its agnatic descent.[1] At the root of perceived power relations among groups are differences not just in the size of their tangible estates but also in the amount of their symbolic capital (cf. R. Tapper 1979: 147; Kressel 1986). As with material capital, symbolic capital has to be accumulated and carefully managed to be effective. This has been recognised by Bourdieu, who notes that patrilateral cousin marriage, 'because it always has the objective effect of reinforcing the integration of the minimal unit and, consequently, its distinctiveness vis-à-vis other units, . . . is likely to be the tactic of groups characterised by a strong desire to assert their distinction' (1977: 57). Bourdieu argues that it achieves this end by the 'affectation of rigour', by 'going one better in purism', by 'stricter observance of the tradition', by 'putting oneself in line with the rule' (ibid.). However, it appears that marriage strategies represent an important aspect of the process of the management of the group's symbolic capital, not through manifesting the actors' adherence to the proclaimed ideal, but because, within the cultural system of expressed marriage preferences and the acknowledged right of men to marry specific women, each marriage becomes a symbolic expression of the recognition of agnatic relationships. A logical corollary of this symbolic aspect of marriage is its ability to produce the very relationships of which it is a symbolic expression. I want to argue further that, since agnatic solidarity (as the most important aspect of the group's symbolic capital) is the cultural expression of the group's power, this solidarity produces the very power of which it is an expression. In this logically-articulated system of cultural meanings of power, agnation and marriage, the marriage strategies constitute the key element in its continuing production.

Status and marriage choices

Many students of close agnatic marriages in the Middle East have been content to calculate their frequency in the studied population from synchronic census. However, some anthropologists have paid attention to, or at least hinted at, the fact that the ratio of close agnatic marriages is uneven among different agnatic groups within the studied society or community,[2] or that it differs or fluctuates over time.[3] Others, although not specifically concerned with the uneven ratio of marriages within different agnatic groups, have nevertheless collected data which indicates it.

In his early writing, Barth predicted that a high frequency of FBD marriages would be associated with a developed lineage organisation in which the lineage and its segments played an important role in armed conflict, and that it would be appreciably lower in villages with a different type of organisation (1953: 68–72; 1954: 167–9).[4] This positive correlation between the power of the lineage, emphasis on agnation and the frequency of patrilateral parallel cousin marriages has subsequently been shown to obtain even in villages of sedentary agriculturalists.

Among the sedentary Pakhtun in Kunar, Afghanistan, a relatively low concentration of land correlates with the solidarity and cohesion of lineage segments as political groups, and the high occurence of patrilateral parallel cousin marriages is charateristic of the politically dominant lineage segments. In the third generation descended from a locally prominent leader, 64 per cent of men and 75 per cent of women were married to patrilateral parallel cousins from their lineage segment. In the fourth generation, this pattern was continued, and 45 per cent of the segment members married patrilateral parallel cousins. The exogamous marriages were with members of five different lineage segments. In the third generation of members of a segment founded by a man who failed to gain local prominence, only 27 per cent of men were married to patrilateral parallel cousins; the exogamous marriages of the members of this segment were made to nine different lineage segments (Christensen 1982: 42). The emergence of new segments is manifested in a fairly high incidence of intra-segment marriages (ibid.: 49). The Pakhtun are clearly aware that marriages can increase or maintain the symbolic capital of the whole descent group and not only of its constituent households. Such awareness is indicated by the fact that the leaders of wealthy and politically influential descent segments control the marriage strategies of the segment members in spite of the proclaimed ideal that it is the male household heads who choose the future spouses of their sons and daughters (ibid.: 55).

In his study of a Shi'ite village in southern Lebanon (1963), Peters shows that a high incidence of close agnatic marriages correlates positively with wealth and rank, and with the importance ascribed to agnatic descent. The Learned Families, as they call themselves, own most of the land in the village and dominate its political life. They trace descent from an ancestor five generations removed, and the notion of this descent validates their position in the village. The peasants, on the other hand, do not reckon patrilineal descent beyond two or three ascending generations. The ratio of patrilateral cousin marriages and other intra-group marriages is considerably higher among the Learned Families than among the peasants.[5]

Similarly, in Buuri al Lamaab village in the Sudan, the occurrence of patrilateral parallel cousin marriages is highest in the most numerous lineage, which is dominant in the village in terms of status and power and has a more distinct identity than the other lineages (Barclay 1964: 81, 87, 121, 131). Virtually the same situation obtains in a Maronite village in the Chouf in Lebanon, and in Arab villages in the lower Galilee of Israel. There, again, the incidence of patrilateral parallel cousin and other intra-lineage marriages is highest in the largest lineages, which contain the principal landowners and are the most important in terms of prestige and power (Cresswell 1976: 104–6; Rosenfeld 1968: 152–7). In a Zikri Baluch fishing community in Pakistan, descendants from the village founder hold the hereditary village headmanship and are economically distinguished from other villagers by their joint ownership of dry-crop land. The percentage of close agnatic marriages contracted in the two generations descended from the village founder is much higher than among the rest of the villagers (Pastner 1979: 38–40; 1981: 311, 316, n. 12).

Antoun's data from Kufr al-Ma village in Jordan convey a similar picture. Of the three main clans in the village (Beni Yasin, Beni Dumi and Beni ʿAmr), the Beni Yasin adhere more strongly than the other two to their patrilineal ideology. They base the superiority of their status within the village on the purity of their descent from one common ancestor, which they contrast with the mixed origin of the other two clans; and they display their unity to a greater extent than do either of the other two clans (Antoun 1972: 88, 103). Although Antoun's charts of the observable marriage pattern were constructed for a different purpose, they show that the occurrence of marriages between patrilateral parallel cousins among various lineages of Beni Yasin (charts 10–14) is distinctly higher than among the lineages of the other two clans (charts 9 and 15).

In his analysis of the marriage pattern in Arab villages in Israel, Cohen provides convincing evidence of the Arabs' awareness of the symbolic meaning of specific marriage choices. Speaking of marriages between different hamulas, he points out that 'the most important index of social ranking in terms of prestige in these Arab villages is the movement of women in marriage between groups ... "Take from the inferior but never give him", says a local proverb.' Each contracted marriage is consequently a symbolic expression of the relative status of the families or wider kinship groups of the spouses: wife-givers are inferior to wife-takers (Cohen 1965: 90). Any hamula attempting to attain a higher social prestige than others in the village has to oppose the marriage of its women to men from other hamulas, for any such marriage is tantamount to a symbolic expression of its inferior status. In a situation where each hamula tries to assert its social prestige as a basis for attaining greater political power, this symbolic significance of the marriage union militates against inter-hamula marriages. A hamula which does not want to admit to its inferior status has to prevent the marriage of its women to outsiders.

The preference for marriage of a woman from a group of lower status to a man from a group of higher status gives meaning to the match as a symbolic expression of the relative status of both spouses. However, the increase in in-hamula marriages is not merely a consequence of the conscious effort to prevent the occurrence of inter-hamula marriages, as has already been argued in the preceding chapter, the in-hamula marriages are symbolically significant in their own right.

Marriages as signs of closeness

In most anthropological writing on the Middle East, there is a conspicuous lack of information on actors' own reasons underlying their observable marriage choices, which makes it rather difficult to prove positively that it is the symbolic meaning of close agnatic marriages that is manipulated by the actors themselves in their marriage strategies. Nevertheless, in those instances where at least some information on actors' own models is provided, it is possible to show that the existing marriage strategies can be explained if preferential in-marriages are seen as symbolic expressions of close agnatic connection between the spouses. Asad provides an account of the models which the Kababish hold, and for this reason I now turn to a brief consideration of his ethnography.

Kababish

The widest category of agnates among the Kababish is the primary subdivision of the tribe called *gabila* (clan). It is a unit which consists of descendants through the male line of a putative single common ancestor (*jid*). Each *gabila* is divided into named subdivisions (subclans) called either *furu'* (sing. *fara'*) or *khashm biyut* (sing. *khashm bayt*) (Asad 1970: 104; the figures in parentheses in this section refer to pages in this text).

Marriages as signs of closeness

Neither *gabila* nor *fara'* has any corporate identity (143); the only exception are the Awlad Fadlallah, a subclan of the Nurab clan headed by the tribal chief (Nazir) himself. Whereas other subclans are dispersed, all the Awald Fadlallah, with the exception of those temporarily absent, live together with their sevants, ex-slaves and clients in a single camp community which migrates together (180 ff.). All its members enjoy certain economic privileges: they are exempted from animal tax and tribute, which all the other Kababish have to pay, and they have a right to prior use of specific pastures (183). Awlad Fadlallah, who form the core of this camp community, are 'a privileged corporate group possessing a monopoly of political power and authority within the tribe' (158). They are referred to as *ahl as-sulta* ('the people of the authority') (195). This designation expresses the fact that the members of Awlad Fadlallah have effective control over the means of public administration through holding the senior offices vested historically in the Nazir's lineage; that they carry influence and prestige with the central government; that they dispose of a traditional client following from which they recruit their personal messengers, accredited agents, clerks and other minor office-holders; and also that they possess the economic resources which enable them to devote themselves fully to their administrative and judicial activities. As *ahl as-sulta*, 'the Awlad Fadlallah are one': they are all kept informed in case of a political confrontation with another tribe or with an official of the central government. The exclusiveness of Awlad Fadlallah and the degree of their internal cohesion in relation to the rest of the Kababish is conspicuous. It is based on their corporate privileges and on the payment or receipt of blood money involving the whole lineage (195–6).

Although all Awlad Fadlallah are collectively referred to as *alh as-sulta*, the power is not equally distributed among them. They are internally divided into eight genealogical segments (*'ailats*), which trace their descent in the agnatic line from sons or grandsons of Fadlallah al-Bay, Nazir of the Kababish around 1870 (196). It is the Nazir's own segment (Ali at-Tom) which monopolises the means of political administration over the entire Kababish tribe: nearly all household heads within this segment hold more than one important administrative or judicial office (199). Members of other segments are barred from access to political privileges which members of the Nazir's segment enjoy, and of which the most important is the eligibility for succession to the nazirate and other senior offices of authority, defined in terms of close agnatic connection to the incumbents.

The high degree of integration of the Awlad Fadlallah is not only based on their corporate privileges, but 'on another level the cohesion also finds expression in the very high rate of marriages contracted within the lineage' (195–6). The rate of marriage within the Awlad Fadlallah subclan is higher than within other subclans (205) (61.1 per cent as against some 58 per cent for other subclans, although the figures are not strictly comparable: cf. 196, 205, 251).

Obviously, intermarriages within the subclan create ties of affinity and matrilateral kinship among its members. Admittedly, close cognatic relationships affect the behaviour in many situations (105 ff., 109) and 'distant agnates never exhibit active solidarity unless they are also close kin' (106). The norm of agnatic solidarity is, however, clearly expressed. 'The closer the agnatic link, the Kababish say, the stronger the sense of obligation between kin: the strongest and most explicit agnatic links outside the elementary family being those between a man and his collaterals of the first degree (i.e. father's siblings and father's brother's children). It is said to be shameful, for example, for a man not to go to the aid of his father's brother's sons when they are attacked ("for were their fathers not brothers, sons of the same father?") though no such obligation arises if more distant agnates are involved' (104). All members of a given clan regard one another as *awlad 'am* (lit. father's brother's sons), and sometimes also use the word *akhwan* (lit. brothers) to indicate their common agnatic origin. '"*Kulluna awlad 'am – kulluna wahid*" they say, "All of us are agnatic cousins – we are all one"' (104). The degree of closeness between various *awlad 'am* is determined by their agnatic genealogy: 'the explanation is sometimes volunteered that since the *jid* of the subclan is more recent than the *jid* of the clan, the descendants of the former are closer to one another than those of the latter, and that the closest of all – on the same principle – are one's father's brother's children' (104). Marriages between them are seen as particularly suitable, and the right of a man to marry his FBD is recognised (58–9).

There is no evidence that, when ideologically asserting their unity, the Awlad Fadlallah imply that they are 'one' because they are intermarried, and connected through ties of cognatic kinship. For the Awlad Fadlallah themselves, their cohesion obviously rests on their agnatic closeness; and their intermarriages, I would suggest, like those of the hamula members in Arab villages in Israel, are symbolic pronouncements about this closeness. They contribute to Awlad Fadlallah's cohesion by symbolically expressing the close agnatic links among them, on which their unity *vis-à-vis* other Kababish is based.

This symbolic meaning of close agnatic marriages upholds the Awlad Fadlallah's own models of their lineage. The members of Ali at-Tom segment effectively hold the political authority which is ideologically seen as vested in the Awlad Fadlallah lineage as a whole (184). In line with this asserted ideology, they stress that the entire Awlad Fadlallah are one; they see Awlad Fadlallah as a 'basically homogeneous group whose genealogical segments have little practical significance' (201). This, according to Asad, may 'be seen as a recognition of the fact that their support is potentially drawn from the entire lineage, and that the prizes for which they contend are linked to the leadership of the lineage as a whole rather than to any part of it' (203). They invoke what Asad calls a legitimacy model of the Awlad Fadlallah lineage (201).

The members of the segments formed by the sons of Muhammad at-Tom, the brother of the former Nazir, are not in a position to compete directly for power (203), being ineligible for succession to the nazirate and other senior offices of authority monopolised by Ali at-Tom segment. Compared with the men of Ali at-Tom segment, they have relatively little wealth and power (203). They are, nevertheless, genealogically close to them and see themselves as belonging to the same prestige group (203); they hold what Asad calls a prestige model of Awlad Fadlallah (201): 'We, the children of Shaikh Ali and Shaikh Muhammad at-Tom, are the *ahl al-mulk* [the people of sovereignty], the *ahl an-nahas* [the people of the copper drums symbolising the Nazir's traditional authority]. All the others [i.e. other segments], they are far away, they don't count' (201).

The legitimacy model of Awlad Fadlallah rests on the premise of close agnatic ties binding together all Awlad Fadlallah irrespective of their segment membership. To substantiate this model, Ali at-Tom have to treat all Awlad Fadlallah as their close agnates, to demonstrate that all of them are one. If, as I have suggested, the recognition of a man's right to marry his agnatic cousin amounts to the recognition of a close agnatic connection between them, the marriage strategies of Awlad Ali at-Tom should become, for them, the means of upholding the view that close agnatic relations exist among themselves and other Awlad Fadlallah. In other words, their marriage strategies should be the means of upholding their legitimacy model, which rests on the acceptance of this view. Obviously, any intermarriages between Awlad Ali at-Tom and other Awlad Fadlallah are symbolic expressions of the existence of close agnatic connections among them, and thus uphold the legitimacy model. Any intermarriages between Awlad Ali at-Tom and Awlad Muhammad at-Tom uphold, at the same time, the prestige model of Awlad Fadlallah which is held by the members of Muhammad at-Tom segment and grounded in the premise of their close agnatic ties with Ali segment. It is significant, in this respect, that 'of the nineteen marriages contracted between the children of Shaikh Ali at-Tom and other Awlad Fadlallah, eleven were with members of the Muhammad at-Tom *'ailat*, and the remaining eight with three other *'ailats*' (204–5).

Although all these marriages are instrumental in upholding *both* existing models, not all of them are of equal significance in upholding *either* the legitimacy *or* the prestige model. Their differing significance derives from the fact that it is the man who has a right to marry his FBD and that it is thus the man, or his father or agnates, who initiate the marriage strategy. Given that the maintenance of the legitimacy model is in the interest of Awlad Ali at-Tom, and the maintenance of the prestige model is in the interest of Awlad Muhammad at-Tom, we should predict that Ali at-Tom men would tend to marry women from as many segments of Awlad Fadlallah as possible, to substantiate their legitimacy model; while Awlad Muhammad at-Tom, who hold the prestige model, would prefer marriages with Ali at-Tom women to marriages with agnatically equally close women from other segments.

There is no information available on the marriage strategies of Awlad Muhammad at-Tom to test the accuracy of this prediction; moreover, the number of marriages contracted by Awlad Ali at-Tom is too small to be statistically conclusive as an indication of existing trends. These difficulties notwithstanding, it still seems to be significant that the pattern of marriages contracted by Awlad Ali at-Tom approximates its predictable shape.

I was able to identify only ten intermarriages between Awlad Ali at-Tom and Awlad Muhammad at-Tom from Asad's diagram of affinal links between Ali at-Tom segment and other Awlad Fadlallah (204). There were nine intermarriages between Awlad Ali at-Tom and three other segments. Of these nineteen marriages, seven were contracted by Awlad Ali at-Tom women and twelve by men (seven men married Muhammad at-Tom women, two Musa women, two Salih women and one a Balal woman). The strategy of Awlad Ali at-Tom men, to marry women from as many segments of Awlad Fadlallah as possible, is thus clearly visible.

The unity of the Awlad Fadlallah is asserted through their agnatic genealogy. However, the notion of common agnation has to be perpetually revalidated to be kept in existence. Awlad Fadlallah maintain the notion of agnation by indicating its continuing importance through their marriages. It is the notion of close agnation which motivates their marriages; these marriages in turn can then be read as signs that a close agnatic link between the spouses has been recognised, and hence that it exists.

Marriages as signs of difference or unity

Among the Kababish, marriage is clearly 'one of the principal opportunities to conserve, increase, or (by misalliance) diminish the capital of authority conferred by strong integration' (Bourdieu 1977: 65). Marriage can, however, increase this capital not only by confirming the existing agnatic links, or by strengthening those which were only vaguely recognised, but also by creating them where none existed previously. This may again best be shown with a specific ethnography.

Arab village in Lower Galilee

The lineage with the highest prestige and economic and political power in the Arab village in Lower Galilee (lineage A) had a conspicuously higher intra-lineage marriage ratio than any other lineage in the village (Rosenfeld 1968: 254). Nevertheless, thirteen women of this lineage married into four other lineages (lineages B) of the twenty-three present in the village, and six women married into two other prestigious lineages (lineages C) in the village. Of the thirty-one women from other lineages in the village who married men of the powerful lineage A, fifteeen came from the weak lineages B and nine from the other two prestigious lineages C. The four lineages B commonly used the name of the powerful lineage A, and in the minds of the villagers were considered to be part of it (ibid.: 255). Obviously implied in these considerations is the idea that A and B must share common agnatic descent, and I would suggest again that it is the symbolic significance of specific marriages that produces this assumption of common agnation. The agnation-creating potential of these marriages derives from the dialectical relationship between the amount of symbolic capital on which the group's power rests and the marriage of the group's members: in addition to the power of a group being sustained or produced through the marriages of its members, marriages themselves may acquire a meaning from the perceived differences of prestige and power among the groups.

The way in which marriages acquire such a meaning may be understood against a background of shared cultural notions, most particularly the fact that in Galilee villages, as generally elsewhere in the Middle East,[6] the movement of women in marriage defines the relative status of individual groups in that the wife-takers are superior or equal to wife-givers.[7] As in Kangra, contracted marriages acquire their meaning as indices of the relative status of different groups because what is immutable is not the respective status of the groups but 'rather the abstract principle that wife-takers rank higher than the wife-givers, and that those who exchange women on a symmetrical basis are equals. What happens is that the status of the male line is constantly being readjusted to take account of the prestige of its recent alliances' (Parry 1979: 204).

This shared knowledge, together with the perceived differences in the prestige and power of individual lineages, is drawn upon to endow specific marriages in Galilee villages with meaning. I wish to argue on the one hand that marriages between A and B and A and C acquire different meanings because of the power differences between B (weak lineages) and C (powerful lineages), and on the other hand that they are instrumental in producing the existing knowledge about the relations of A and B and A and C.

Let us dispose of A and C first. As they are both powerful lineages, intermarriages between them are between equals. Since both lineages are both wife-givers and wife-takers, neither lineage jeopardises its status by giving women to and taking women from the other; in consequence, intermarriages between them do not connote common agnation.

Intermarriages between A and B are different, and they are of specific interest because of their agnation-creating effect. When women of B marry men of A, the relative symbolic capital of A and B is confirmed; it is perfectly understandable within existing cultural notions that men marry women of inferior status and that inferior lineages, having no symbolic capital to protect and no strength to protect it, concede their women to a superior lineage. But marriages of A women to B men negate A's prestige and power. This contradiction is resolved by constructing a notion of common agnation of A and B, however tenuous or remote, drawing on the cultural knowledge that marriage between agnates connotes the equality of their status. Marriages between women of A and men of B make cultural sense, and hence can be allowed and tolerated – as indeed they are – only within this context; at the same time, it is these marriages themselves which produce this very context.

If my explanation is correct, it would follow that B did not ally themselves with A to increase their prestige, but that A incorporated them through their own marriage strategies, aiming to increase their symbolic capital through increasing their numerical strength. This explanation is of course only speculative; the available ethnography is silent on the reasons for B aligning themselves with A, and no description is available of the process through which this alignment occurred and the way in which it was rationalised. However, the hypothesis can be tested in future fieldwork.

The next point is equally speculative because of the lack of necessary ethnographic information (which again could be gathered in future fieldwork). The agnation-affecting marriages are of course only a part of the totality of marriages occurring in any given population. To be effective in promoting agnatic solidarity (by confirming or narrowing existing agnatic ties, or possibly even by creating them where they did not exist previously), one would assume that they would have to be clearly marked so that they could be discriminated from other non-marked marriages. If this were not the case, either all marriages, or else none of them, would affect the notions of agnation. It does not seem, however, that there is any semantic differentiation between agnation-connoting and other marriages; only exchange marriages, whether between agnates or non-agnates, are semantically differentiated from ordinary marriages contracted through the transfer of bridewealth. However, it is widely reported from all over the Middle East that there is a considerable reduction in the amount of bridewealth transferred in marriages between agnates, their lesser cost often being considered as an important incentive. I would suggest that it is the amount of requested or actually-transferred bridewealth that signifies the presence or absence of an agnatic link between spouses, and that it is from this symbolic significance that bridewealth derives its meaning in the context of the Middle Eastern marriage pattern. If full bridewealth is not demanded, the presence of an agnatic link is signalled, whether or not such a link has been acknowledged before. On the other hand, requesting full bridewealth in the case of agnatic connection between the spouses signifies the denial of the agnatic link, like the refusal to give one's daughter in marriage to a man who has a right to her due to his agnatic relationship. Requesting or demanding full or reduced bridewealth is thus the main means through which the imposition of particular meanings on particular marriages is manipulated.

Despite this rather speculative conclusion, I hope that the data discussed in this chapter have indicated the positive correlation between the power of the group, the emphasis on agnation and the frequency of patrilateral parallel cousin and other intra-group marriages. The cultural logic which underlies and generates the observable correlation derives from the fact that, while the agnatic ideology justifies, validates or legitimises the group's solidarity, cohesion, corporateness, status, prestige or power, it is the close agnatic marriages that are instrumental in producing the notion of agnation by being, at the same time, its most important symbolic expression.

Notes to Chapter 4

1   In view of the criticisms of the analyses of Middle Eastern social structures carried out in terms of the lineage model (Peters 1976: 32; Geertz 1979: 316, 377, n. 1), this generalisation requires clarification. The cultural importance of agnation, which is postulated here as one of the common features of Middle Eastern societies, does not imply 'a cultural model for group formation which is based on a systematic elaboration of the chain of father-son links into a branching tree form, with group segmentation programmed to occur at each forking point' (Geertz 1979: 348). It merely implies that importance is ascribed by the actors to the tracing of descent through a chain of patrifilial links to a common ancestor, and to the tracing of relations through men. In this sense, it is a wider concept than that of the 'segmentary patrilineal lineage', and while the latter concept inevitably implies the former, the former does not necessarily imply the latter. Stress is often laid on agnatic links between members of groups which cannot be classified as segmentary lineages. For example, the members of patronymic groups in Arab villages in Israel clearly conceptualise their relationships in agnatic terms (Cohen 1965: 3, 107, 109). The same applies to patronymic associations in Morocco, whose members are recruited on the basis of genealogical and patronage ties and which, as Geertz convincingly

shows, cannot be seen as groups that are 'closely bounded and ordered according to distinct principles that in some simple way could distinguish members from nonmemebers, in accordance with recognition or nonrecognition of specific kinship ties' (Geertz 1979: 316). The cultural emphasis on agnation within the patronymic association is indicated by the fact that the patronym is the name of an ancestor the descent from whom is traced, or presumed to have occurred, through a chain of patrifilial links (ibid.: 341–2); the naming convention is a patrifiliatively-transmitted chain of patronyms (ibid.: 356); the kinship terms for close agnates (FB, FBS) are used to refer to the members of the patronymic association, and the 'sons or descendants of fathers' brothers' is the most common way of referring to the patronymic association as a whole (ibid.: 347–8); kinship connections are traced exclusively through men, with daughters, mothers and wives not being spontaneously mentioned (even by women) (ibid.: 350); 'maternal kinsmen, despite their emotional importance and their genealogical proximity, are not often thought of as a homogeneous category of persons in the same way as are the paternal kinsmen who form the core of the patronymic association' (ibid.: 357).

Equating the expressed agnatic ideology with actual social patterns is probably responsible for the fact that numerous authors have formulated their ethnographic descriptions in terms of a lineage model. As I am not primarily concerned with actual principles of group affiliation, but rather with the cultural conceptualisation of existing groups, the terms employed by authors of particular ethnographic descriptions ('lineage', 'descent group', 'hamula', etc.) are retained when I refer to such groups. When the term 'agnatic group' is supplied, it refers solely to the culturally-expressed ideology of group membership (Scheffler 1966: 546) rather than the actual principles of affiliation (see Bates and Rassam 1983: 195).

2 Barth 1954; Peters 1963; Barclay 1964; Rosenfeld 1968; Asad 1970; Cohen 1974: 115; Cresswell 1976; Meeker 1976: 395; Bourdieu 1977: 204, n. 54; Pitt-Rivers 1977: 121; Pastner 1979; 1981; Geertz 1979: 324, 374–5, 386–90; Anderson 1982: 11–12; Tillion 1983: 110, 127.
3 Chelhod 1964; Cohen 1965; Aswad 1971; Rosenfeld 1976; Christensen 1982.
4 Chelhod (1964) similarly noted that the ratio of endogamous marriages, which is higher in nomadic tribes in a state of constant war than among sedentary populations, tends to rise when there are threats of war or conflict.
5 This statement is based on figures Peters gives (1963: 177–9), although he himself says that 'first and second parallel cousin marriage among peasants is as high as it is among the Learned Families, but the incidence of third or fourth parallel cousin marriages is very much lower' (ibid.: 189).
6 Cohen 1965: 90; Randolph and Coult 1968: 94; Rosenfeld 1968: 253, 255, 257; Gellner 1969: 140, 182, 191; Bourdieu 1977: 67; Christensen 1982: 53; Abu Zahra 1982: 146, 151, 152; Cole 1984: 179, 183; Kressel 1986: 176–9.
7 The Shahsevan are again an exception to this (R. Tapper 1979: 144).

Chapter 5

Preference for FBD marriage in context

My investigation of parallel cousin marriage was triggered off by the assertion that it is sociologically inexplicable, or that it is futile to look for one single sociological explanation of it. In this essay, I have tried to show that what leads to this pessimistic conclusion is the consideration of this type of marriage as an action which can be understood in its 'situational' context (Keesing 1972: 18). It has, I hope, also indicated that the contextualisation of the studied phenomenon, more than anything else, determines the analyst's success or failure in explaining it. In this respect, 'context' appears to be the most important concept in the anthropologists' conceptual armoury, to which all the other concepts (like function or meaning, for example) are subordinate. It may seem that the phenomena we try to explain determine how we perceive the context in which they are situated. But in fact what we describe as the relevant context depends not only on the phenomenon as such but also on what we want to know about it. At the same time, the way in which we conceptualise the relevant context determines both the formulation of what we see as problems to be explained and what we accept as reasonable explanations (Gellner 1970: 41). In my view, the whole intellectual history of anthropology bears witness to this. However else the conceptual shifts in anthropology might be envisaged, they can be seen as shifts in the conceptualisation of what constitutes the relevant context of the phenomena which anthropologists try to explain.

Conceptualisations of context

For Frazer, a global culture, differentiated only through the stages of savagery and civilisation (Strathern 1987: 263), was the relevant context for the beliefs, customs and ritual practices whose rationality and motivation he tried to elucidate. When his approach was later rejected by the functionalists, the main charge levelled against him was that he removed the studied phenomena from their context. In the way in which it was formulated, the charge implied that phenomena belong intrinsically to a specific context, from which they must not be removed if they are to be properly understood, and that Frazer simply chose to ignore this inherent contextual fit.

When, in their turn, the functionalists' assumptions ceased to be universally shared, it became apparent that context is in no sense 'given', and that what Frazer actually did was to remove the studied phenomena from the context in which they made sense to the functionalists: the context of the social life in which the phenomena function. This consists, on the one hand, of all actions and practices observable in a given society and the beliefs which inform them; and, on the other hand, of the multiplicity of ties which bind together their performers within the system of social relations constituting a functioning whole which can be conveniently set against other such systems for comparative purposes. As Strathern points out, 'the organising analystical ideas of the anthropologists were themselves contextualised by putting into *their* social context the indigenous ideas through which people organised their experiences' (1987: 259). The practice of comparing beliefs, customs and practices within the context of a world culture was replaced by the practice of comparing contexts.

It would probably be futile to speculate as to whether it was the rejection of Frazer's methodology which led to the recognition of a different context as relevant for the phenomena he tried to explain, or the recognition of a different context which led to the rejection of his methodology and his style of explanation. The role ascribed to fieldwork in functionalist anthropology would favour the latter view. But whatever the cause and whatever the effect, the novel context and the novel mode of explanation went hand in hand. The very shift from the Frazerian emphasis on notions (belief) to the emphasis on action (ritual) was indicative of the recognition of new contextual relevance.

The subsequent demise of structural-functionalism, and its replacement by various kinds of interpretative approach, can again be envisaged as a shift in the conceptualisation of the relevant context. Irrespective again of how else the shift may be conceptualised, it was to a great extent accomplished through privileging the system of signs and symbols (culture) over the system of interaction and social relations (society). For example, myth is no longer understood as a charter for social action but as an attempt at highlighting and deflecting basic conceptual contradictions; witchcraft is no longer understood as a device for coping with tensions arising from living together in society but as one of many possible ways in which human conduct can be morally evaluated (Crick 1976: 109–29); and so on.

Conceptualisations of context

The change from the concern with what institutions do to the concern with how they are culturally constructed is underpinned by the change in the conceptualisation of the context in which they should be properly placed. The postmodern phase in social anthropology, which manifests itself in the rise of reflexive anthropology, critial anthropology, semantic anthropology, semiotic anthropology and poststructuralism (Crick 1985: 71), is characterised by conscious 'playing with context' (Strathern 1987: 263–70).

On this reading of the changing theoretical fashions in social anthropology, context is and always has been the key anthropological concept. This has been stressed by, among many others, Gellner, who repeatedly made the point that the distinguishing feature of most social anthropology was its stress on context in analysis (1970; 1973a; 1973b). Considering its importance in any kind of anthropological inquiry, it is remarkable to what extent the definition and delineation of context has always been regarded as unproblematic. While other key concepts received close scrutiny from time to time (for meaning, see Hobart 1982), the notion of context has remained virtually unanalysed. Although different anthropological approaches differed widely in their views about what constitutes the proper context in which the phenomena should be placed to be understood and explained, they have always treated context as a 'given' or self-evident construct. Maybe anthropologists were able to go on with their job precisely because the key concept of the discipline was treated as unproblematic. Yet, in a sense, it is the most problematic of all the concepts anthropologists employ. Ultimately, of course, the whole world is the context for anything. But such wide conceptualisation of context is obviously neither manageable nor very practical. The world somehow has to be divided up to arrive at a manageable context into which to place a phenomenon to make sense of it. There are, of course, many different ways in which the world can be divided, and some are more useful than others. This has been well recognised in the discussion about 'relevant context', a phrase which implies that there are many contexts into which a phenomenon may be placed but that not all of them matter. It also suggests that there is no inherent relationship between a phenomenon and its context. Phenomena may be put into different contexts, or seen in different contexts, of which only some are relevant.

If there is no intrinsic relationship between a phenomenon and its context, there is an intrinsic relationship between the meaning of a phenomenon and its context. All theories of meaning acknowledge this relationship in one way or another (see Hobart 1982). This has, of course, always been commonsensically recognised. The charge that the intended meaning of an utterance has been altered or deliberately distorted by quoting it 'out of context' rests on the recognition that context is essential for the correct understanding of the meaning. The same utterance carries different meanings in different contexts (Tyler 1978: 31), and different utterances carry the same meaning in the same context. Nothing has meaning in isolation, and meaning and context are inseparable. Gellners's observation along these lines that 'the range of context, and the manner in which the context is seen, necessarily affect interpretation' (1970: 41) has recently prompted Asad to point out that 'the problem is always what kind of context?' (1986: 151).

It has also been recognised that meaning is not simply the result of consensus and a non-problematical agreement about the context into which the phenomenon 'properly' belongs. Meanings are negotiated, challenged, argued about, imposed, altered or reinterpreted to reflect changed circumstances or changed goals and aspirations of individuals and groups. In brief, meanings are subject to manipulation. If meanings are intrinsically context-dependent, any manipulation of meaning involves perforce manipulation of its contextualisation. Such manipulation may be triggered off either by the desire to impose new meaning or to reinterpret the existing meaning of a phenomenon, or by the recognition of a new conceptual domain or a new situation as a context from which the phenomenon derives its significance. In the former case, the relevant context in which to understand the phenomenon is redefined; in the latter case, the perceived meaning of the phenomenon is reinterpreted or, at least, challenged. The former process of the manipulation of meaning is widely resorted to in political practice. The latter process is exemplified by the very history of anthropology, to which I have alluded.

The intrinsic relationship between meaning and context has yet further implications for the conceptualisation of the relevant context which is germane to the present discussion. If phenomena may be differently interpreted or ascribed different meanings by the analysts and the actors, it logically follows that relevant contexts may also be differently defined by them. As Hobart recently pointed out, 'in adopting academically fashionable criteria for selecting relevant contexts in preference to those used by the participants themselves, we may be guilty simultaneously of an act of distortion and a subtle kind of epistemological domination' (1986: 8).

There are at least two ways in which anthropologists can part company with the actors in conceptualising context. The first derives from the fact that the anthropologist's interest in elucidating any phenomenon is always a theorectical one, whereas the actors' interest, if not necessarily directly or strictly a practical one, is always at least partly circumscribed by their practice. The anthropologist's interest is thus qualitatively different from any possible interest of the actors: he/she studies the culture; the actors live it or live by it, they create and recreate it. They may both be interpreting it, but they are interpreting it from different positions and for different purposes. Most importantly, they are interpreting it for different audiences: the actors interpret it for themselves and other members of their culture; the anthropologists interpret it for the members of their own culture or for their fellow anthropologists. The respective interpretations are carried out from vastly different vantage points. Moreover, adopting a specific vantage point always involves a precarious balancing act for the analyst. As an ethnographer, he/she is in the business of elucidating a culture with which he/she became familiar during fieldwork; as an anthropologist, he/she is in the business of contributing to the development of anthropological knowledge and theory. As a result of this dual role, what he/she wants to say about something derives also to a considerable extent from what is perceived as being worth saying about it in terms of the current anthropological theory. Consequently, in numerous subtle ways, the anthropological theory of the day affects the anthropologists' contextualisation of the studied phenomena.

The second way in which the actors' and anthropologists' contextualisations may differ is closely connected with the first. It derives from the fact that anthropologists not only have much more freedom than the actors to put the studied phenomena in a wider range of contexts, but are also in a unique position to create their own context for them. This is the context of their comparative generalisations, to which nobody except anthropologists has access, for it is a context which they define from their position as specialists in crossing cultural boundaries and as translators of cultures.

Hobart recently suggested that 'a serious difficulty in much anthropological argument is that there is no satisfactory theory of context' (1985: 33), and Keesing pointed out some time ago the need for a formal theory of context definition (1970: 447). He argued elsewhere that 'contexts are in our heads, not "out there"', and that 'a "grammar" for creating contexts out of perceived flux must be coded in the brain' (Keesing 1972: 29). To say, then, as Gellner does, that 'there is nothing in the nature of things or societies to dictate visibly just how much context is relevant to any given utterance, or how the context should be described' (1970: 33), does not appear to be accurate. As Asad argues, people learn the skills to discriminate relevant contexts; and 'which context is relevant in different discursive events is something one learns in the course of living' (1986: 149). It is of course often difficult to verbalise this knowledge; and it still remains a mystery 'how the mind/brain encodes and interprets complex spectra of meaning and contextual variation, and how this process can be formally represented' (Keesing 1972: 20). To solve this mystery appears now to be the urgent task of the various disciplines engaged in the study of human cognition. It is unlikely that anthropologists will be able to do this on their own, but their close attention to how the actors contextualise phenomena in the course of their everyday living, and in the process of learning their own culture, should be an important part of this concentrated effort.

Preference for FBD marriage in context

This essay cannot claim to make a contribution to formulating a theory of context definition. However, it pays close attention to how the actors themselves contextualise the preference for marriages with patrilateral cousins. In this respect, it tries to go beyond the traditional consideration of this type of marriage within either the broad context of the system of social action or the equally broad context of culture, not only by considering it in both these wide contexts, as the actors themselves do, but also by formulating more directly relevant specific contexts within which this type of marriage can be seen as functional, and from which the preference for it derives its meaning.

All these immediate contexts are mutually related. In the foregoing discussion of Berti marriage preferences, it has been pointed out that the same meanings are ascribed to different marriage preferences, because different people consider each marriage in different contexts selected from the multiplicity of contexts in which the desirability of any marriage can be evaluated. By the same token, marriages which are the same in terms of genealogical relations between spouses can serve widely different functions depending on which context of relations the actors choose to exploit to their strategic advantage. The fact that 'marriages which are identical as regards genealogy alone...may have different, even opposite meanings and functions' has been clearly recognised by Bourdieu (1977: 48; see also Eickelman 1981: 132). Nevertheless, his conclusion that 'any two marriages between parallel cousins may have nothing in common' (ibid.) does not seem necessarily to follow. Whether they are seen as having anything in common or not depends entirely on which criteria of identity or difference we care to apply to them, i.e. whether we consider as relevant the identity or difference between their instrumental, or their expressive or symbolic aspects.

Throughout the Middle East, FBD marriage is a 'marked' marriage, consistently perceived as special and, in particular significant ways, different from other marriages. It is, of course, its symbolic aspect which 'marks' it; and I would suggest that, as far as this aspect is concerned, all patrilateral parallel cousin marriages can be seen as identical, for they always express the existence and recognition of the significance of particular relations, irrespective of the strategy in which they are involved and the particular pragmatic reasons for which they are contracted.

Preference for FBD marriage in context

Underlying the variability of their practical functions lies their unity as a cultural notion.

When the preference for FBD marriage is considered within the context of the cultural notions of which it is a part, it can be seen as meaningful only alongside all other preferences which the actors express. The most important of these are the preferences for marriages with other cousins besides the patrilateral parallel ones. All these preferences relate logically to the low cultural value ascribed to affinity in comparison with kinship, and acquire their meaning as particular expressions of a more general preference: the preference for marriages with kin beyond the range of prohibited degrees as opposed to marriages with strangers. Within this general preference for in-marriages, the preference for marriage with the FBD can be read as a preference for the closest possible kin: marriage between patrilateral parallel cousins is a marriage between agnates who are conceptualised as the closest kin throughout many areas of the Middle East, and are often the only people bound together by ties of 'legal kinship' (Tillion 1983: 37, 74).

As marriage with the FBD is a marriage between agnates, the preference for it acquires meaning as a symbolic expression of the existence of agnatic ties between the spouses. Furthermore, it acquires meaning as a positive affirmation of the importance of these ties. The logical corollary of FBD marriage as a signifier of agnatic ties is its ability not only to reproduce but also to produce them. Because of their symbolic significance, marriages that can be seen as having followed the asserted preference bring the pragmatically-determined relations of cooperation in line with the asserted agnatic ideology, and thus tend to eliminate the perpetually-existing discrepancy between the actual practice and its ideal. In this respect, they are instrumental in producing and reproducing both the asserted ideology and the agnatic solidarity which this ideology prescribes.

The emphasis on kinship and the devaluation of affinity, the recognition of agnatic ties as the closest and most binding ones, the high value placed on agnatic solidarity, and the preference for FBD marriage, are all logically interrelated. The meaning of the asserted preference derives from its place in the context of these interrelated cultural notions, and from the constitutive relationship between this type of marriage and the other elements of the socio-cultural reality in which it occurs. This meaning is not merely that which I described before as 'analytical'; it is ascribed to the asserted preference by the actors themselves. It is precisely this 'cultural' meaning which they strategically manipulate in their effort to acknowledge existing relations and to create new ones through their marriage strategies.

Explaining the preference for FBD marriage as meaningful within the context of the existing cultural notions is not simply an alternative to explaining it in terms of the practical functions which the FBD marriage fulfils. The former explanation is logically prior to the latter, in that it links the preference for FBD with the constitutive elements of the cultural system which any kind of functional explanation has to take for granted, and hence to leave unexplained.

Agnatic solidarity and the metaphor of property

To establish this last point, let us consider the functional explanation that has been advanced most often since the time of Westermarck (1891).[1] It suggests that FBD marriage is preferred because it keeps the property 'in the family'. Specifying the unit that aims at preventing the alienation of its property through out-marriage as 'the family' is at once vague and inaccurate. In fact, what is prevented through FBD marriage is the alienation of the property from the lineage, patronymic group or patrilineal descent line. Instead of being transmitted through the man's daughter to his cognates (typically his daughter's children), the property is preserved for his agnates (typically his brother's son's children). Underlying this 'strategy of heirship' (Goody 1976; 1983) is the ascription of a higher value to agnatic than to cognatic connections; in fact, the strategy makes sense only when agnatic connections are valued more highly than genealogically closer cognatic connections. In this sense, the effort to preserve property in the agnatic line is but a specific expression of a more general value ascribed to agnatic solidarity; and the latter logically precedes the former, in the sense that FBD marriage would not be able to fulfil its alleged function if agnatic solidarity were not highly valued. The notion of agnatic solidarity generates the preference for FBD marriage; but the effect of this marriage in preserving the property in the agnatic line does not generate the notion of agnatic solidarity. To resort to FBD marriage because of its obvious effects makes sense only when the value of agnatic solidarity is already presupposed.

Apart from a preference for marriages between the closest kin beyond the range of prohibited degrees, another preference clearly expressed throughout the Middle East is for marriage between social equals (homogamy), or for marriage of a man of higher rank to a woman of lower rank (hypergamy).[2] Another weakness of the explanation of patrilateral parallel cousin marriage in terms of its economic functions lies in the fact that this kind of reasoning has to divorce the preference for close agnatic marriage from the preference for hypergamous marriages and to consider it independently of the latter. If to preserve the property in the family were the prime objective of the marriage strategy, one would assume that not only the preservation of the family property but also its augmentation would be consistently pursued. Hypogamy and not hypergamy would then be the logical option, for a bride from a higher-ranking, and usually wealthier, group is likely to be better endowed than one from a lower-ranking, and usually poorer, group. By transmitting her property through inheritance to her children, who are members of the group into which she married, she would alienate property from her own group to that of her husband.

It is of course possible that hypogamy could not be practised simply because the wealthier groups oppose this alienation of their property through out-marriage of their women. But more than this seems to be involved in shaping marriage strategies, for the proscription on giving women to men of inferior status is widespread and not limited to groups of higher ranking.

There is no denying that close agnatic marriages are often resorted to because of their obvious economic benefits. But explaining them in terms of this pragmatic function is too specific to constitute a general theory. In many cases, it is also inaccurate; for example, the close agnatic marriage is often the preference of the property-less as much as the propertied (Khuri 1970: 601; Tillion 1983: 105). It is considered an ideal marriage both among those who adhere to the Koranic inheritance and among those who disregard it completely. If property were all that mattered, the latter would clearly have no reason to insist on marriages between close agnates. As a strategy of heirship, marriage of close kin would anyhow seem superfluous, given that polygyny, concubinage and leviratic unions are all available as alternative strategies (Goody 1983).

On the strength of the argument outlined above, it seems more plausible to see FBD marriage as preventing the alienation, not of the group's material property, but of its whole symbolic capital, of which the material property is just one specific manifestation. The expressed ideals of close agnatic marriage and hypergamy or marriage between equals are not determined by any practical function which they may fulfil, but are logically related to another asserted ideal, that of agnatic solidarity. One of the obvious consequences of hypergamy is that a person's agnates, who represent his/her nearest kin, do not rank higher than his/her maternal kin. In the case of a hypogamous marriage, the loyalty of the man's descendants to his own agnatic group may be lost, for they may align with their own mothers' brothers (who rank higher) rather than with their father's brothers or their own agnates (who rank lower). In this respect, hypergamy has the same effect as a close agnatic marriage and positively correlates with the maintenance of the solidarity of the agnatic group over generations. Hypogamy would create a conflict of interests among the members of the youngest generation of the agnatic group, and may result in the possible loss of their loyalty to the group. It would threaten the effective maintenance of the ideology of agnatic solidarity as much as straightforward group exogamy would. It makes sense, then, that close agnatic marriages cease to be seen as desirable, and cease to be practised, not when property loses significance but when the kinship universe ceases to be the main arena of practical action, i.e. when the importance of kinship ties diminishes and the importance of relations with strangers increases (Tillions 1983: 109), and in consequence of this the ideal of agnatic solidarity ceases to be in any way meaningful.

If my argument is correct, and the preference for in-marriages and hypergamy springs from the internal logic of the cultural system that puts high emphasis on kin solidarity, rather than from the pragmatic functions which such marriages can serve, there is one more important problem that has to be addressed: the problem of the actors' statements of reasons for the existence of their marriage preferences. As I noted earlier, many analysts have pointed out that one reason stated by the actors – that marriages between patrilateral parallel cousins prevent the alienation of property from the family – would hold only if the norms of Koranic inheritance were strictly observed. As these are more often disregarded than not, the native statements were rejected as implausible explanations.

Assuming that the actors would not make statements which make no sense to them, to reject these statements as false amounts to an admission on the part of the analyst that he/she has failed to comprehend them in the way they were meant, and in the way the actors themselves comprehend them. This failure derives, in my view, from analytically privileging the context of actual practice over the context of asserted norms which are ideally supposed to govern it, and from considering the reasons given by the actors as plausible or otherwise only within the context of actual practice. Interestingly enough, this is the analytical strategy adopted even by those who, like Khuri (1970), accept the natives' reasons for marriages between parallel cousins as plausible ones. The weakness of this strategy derives from the fact that the normative context cannot be so easily dismissed from consideration: as the preceding discussion has indicated, the actors themselves consider their marriage preferences *both* in the context of actual practice *and* in the context of its normative structure. It is of course the normative context within which marriages acquire their meaning as expressive acts. Given this contextualisation, I would suggest that the full meaning of actors' statements of reasons for their preference for FBD marriages can be grasped only when such marriages are seen not only as instrumental acts but also as expressive or symbolic acts.

As expressive acts, marriages between kin make pronouncements about the value of kinship solidarity; in this respect, they are the language in which the values are expressed. Consequently, the statements which the actors make about them are a language in which language is talked about; they are statements about statements. When making their statements, the actors do of course communicate meaning, and the problem facing the analyst is to decipher it. It seems to me that, in dealing with this problem, we have been directed along the wrong track by following too closely the rigorous methodology of modern linguistics. Instead of seeing too close a parallel between language and culture, and analysing culture as grammar by drawing inspiration from the formal semantic analysis of language, it seems methodologically more profitable to pay closer attention to the way people *use* language to communicate meaning to one another.

We know from our own experience that the meaning of a new world is not ordinarily communicated through giving its explicit semantic definition; we rather learn it through hearing the word applied to particular examples, or occasionally by being given examples of the word's proper use or of specific phenomena as its referents (Sampson 1980: 47–8; Fodor 1975: 153–4). The use of exemplification as a method of communicating meaning is also habitually resorted to in the case of more complex concepts: a student unable to provide a definition of a concept which would adequately circumscribe its meaning typically conveys his/her understanding of the concept's meaning by giving an example of it. When the meaning of a word or concept is communicated in this way, the concept's referent becomes concretised and in consequence that aspect of the referent which is brought into focus becomes narrowed. The concretised referent of the concept is here used figuratively: it is a specific entity standing for a more general class of similar entities, something concrete standing for something abstract, something unique standing for something general, or a part standing for a whole. Instead of communicating meaning in a propositional form, explanations by exemplification rely on its communication in a figurative or symbolic form.

The inability to formulate abstract ideas in propositional form is, of course, general. As Beattie reminded us a long time ago, if everything that is to be communicated could be stated in propositional form, one of the main reasons for resorting to symbolic expression would not exist:

Sociologically, this is the most important thing about symbols; they provide people with a means of representing abstract ideas, often ideas of great importance to themselves, indirectly, ideas which it would be difficult or even impossible for them to represent to themselves directly. We sometimes forget that the capacity for systematic analytical thinking about concepts is the product of several millennia of education and constant philosophizing (1964: 70; see also Skorupski 1976: 41).

I would suggest that the arguments about the implausibility of the actors' stated reasons for their marriage preferences are based on a failure to realise that the actors' statements are figurative or symbolic.

When the actors state that an FBD marriage is a good one because it keeps property in the family, or because it secures for the man the political support of his brother's son, these statements are understood to mean just that; the figurative statements to which the actors resort when they find it difficult to express the more general principle in propositional form are taken literally. It is assumed that they are statements about property or political support, and hence that the actors' concerns with property or political support constitute the reasons for their assertions that FBD marriages are preferable to any other marriages.

It is asserted that some of the actors' stated reasons for their marriage preferences are implausible; but this assertion itself becomes implausible when these statements are understood as communicating not the meaning of marriage preferences as instrumental devices for the manipulation of property or political support, but their meaning as expressions of norms, values and ideals underpinning the relations among kin. When the actors say that marriages between patrilateral cousins are good ones because they keep property in the family or enable a man to mobilise the political support of his brother's son, they employ concrete symbols of property or political loyalties to indicate that such marriages are good because they enable close agnates to share their common interests. The sharing of property or political allegiance is used as a symbol of a more abstract and general notion of sharing common interests, on which the solidarity of close agnates rests. On this reading, the positive values ascribed by the actors to FBD marriages derive not so much from their overtly stated practical effects as from the more general values of which the overtly-stated effects are an exemplification on the level of concrete action: it is not only the sharing of property or political support which is at issue but the more general and abstract values of kinship solidarity, of which sharing property, political support or whatever is merely one concrete instantiation.

Barth's analysis of the determinants of descent-group formation in the Middle East provides a clue to understanding why it is property and political support which seem universally to be seized upon throughout the Middle East as concrete symbols for the abstract values of kinship (or more specifically agnatic) solidarity of which the marriage preferences are an expression. He argues that, with the 'codification of kinship relations as essentially "of the same kind", the range of what will be experienced as *distinctive* for agnates becomes limited', and that 'descent group affairs focus on property and the control of territory: they relate to a particular joint tangible estate' (1973: 17). It is significant in this context that, while the Berti explicitly refer to the political significance of FBD marriages, they do not assert, as many people in the Middle East do, that such marriages keep property in the family. In fact, they emphatically deny that the preference for marriages between kin generally, or between patrilateral parallel cousins specifically, has anything to do with property considerations. Among the Shahsevan, too, 'agnatic cousin marriage is never practised in order to keep the property in the family', and cousin marriages of all types are often praised for 'keeping the family together' (R. Tapper 1979: 141). Among these peoples, in the absence of joint family estate, the common fund of property cannot be utilised as a symbol of the mutuality of interests among kin and as a figurative expression of the norms, values and ideals of kinship solidarity.

In-marriages and the integration of society

A theme that has emerged recurrently in the course of this study is the low cultural value ascribed to affinity in comparison with kinship, which at the social-structural level finds its expression in the reluctance to establish affinal relationships. We are dealing here with a system opposite to the exogamous system, which emphasises marriages alliances and places a high value on affinity – at least in the patterning of actual interactions if not asserting it ideologically, although the latter too is very often the case in the systems which proscribe marriages among kin. This opposition is not, of course, so clearly manifest at the social-structural level. For obvious demographic reasons, a system which completely proscribed marriages between strangers would be unworkable in practice: the universe of marriageable women would in many cases be so limited that a number of individuals would have to remain forever unmarried. The statistical analyses of the marriage pattern of Middle Eastern communities have shown, however, that even at the level of actual action the system very often strives towards its fullest possible expression, in that the practice of marriages between close kin is carried out to the very limits of demographic possibility. Even though the opposition between proscribing marriages between kin and favouring them over marriages with strangers cannot be fully expressed at the level of concrete action, it is clearly articulated at the level of existing cultural notions. The preference for FBD marriage is but one of these notions; the different values ascribed to kinship and affinity are another.

Proscription of marriage between kin and preference for marriage between kin are two culturally-possible ways of defining marriageable women. The consequences of the first alternative for the integration of society have been widely accepted as reasons for its world-wide preponderance. However, the integrative effect of the system of exchange of women between groups is achieved at the expense of compromising the group's solidarity. The loyalties of those who are members of the group of one of their parents by virtue of their descent, and who are linked to the group of their other parent by what Fortes (1953) called 'complementary filiation', are inevitably divided, and it is precisely their divided loyalty through which the society's integration is maintained in the face of inter-group conflict (Gluckman 1956).

The second alternative does not compromise the group's solidarity, for it effectively prevents its members from developing a loyalty to any group other than their own. In many cases, this not only an unforeseen consequence of in-marriage but a conscious motivation for it. The Berti mention it as one of the reasons for marriages between kin, and the Arab villagers on the Israeli–Jordanian border explain their preference for such marriages by saying that children born of them have no divided loyalties because 'they have the same men as their father's brothers and mother's brothers, and their loyalties therefore "remain within their camp"' (Cohen 1974: 116). In Sidi Ameur village in Tunisia, the relationship between FBD marriage and the solidarity of agnates is expressed in the saying 'may God not decrease the number of our men and women' (Abu Zahra 1982: 73).

In stressing different values, i.e. the group's solidarity on the one hand, and on the other hand the creation of relations between different groups through links of affinity and kinship which mutually bind their members, the systems of in-marriage and out-marriage opt for two different strategies for coping with problems facing any society (for the discussion of the integrative aspects of the two systems see Irons 1975: 133–4). The system of in-marriage obviously misses out on the integrative advantages of the system of out-marriage, which is precisely the reason why it has been so puzzling, and why it has occasionally been seen as a kind of aberration. It is, nevertheless, a viable system which has solved in its own way the problem of the integration of the wider society. This has been achieved not only by means of genealogies (Murphy and Kasdan 1959: 23) or patrilineal descent (Patai 1965: 347–8), but also through the exchange of specialised goods and services produced or performed by members of endogamous groups and strata (Cole 1973; 1984: 172, 184), or through the ethnic-based division of labour (Coon 1958: 3). For demographic reasons, the ideal of in-marriage can never be fully realised in behavioural practice, and therefore the alliance through marriage between members of different groups inevitably contributes to the integration of the wider society at the level of its practice, even if this role is denied at the level of the proclaimed ideal. In the overall effect achieved through the inevitable compromise between the asserted ideal and its limited possibility of realisation in practice, the system of in-marriage can be seen as having distinct organisational advantages over the system of out-marriage. It manages, as it were, to preserve the advantageous aspects of both logical alternatives.

This may indeed be the reason for the widespread occurrence of in-marriage in the early civilisations of the Middle East, the Mediterranean and Europe (Goody 1983).

FBD marriage and Islam

In Europe, from the fourth century onward, marriage between close kin became prohibited by the Christian Church (Goody 1983); and, with a few notable exceptions, preference for marriages between close kin, and particularly close agnates, is nowadays confined to the Middle East and adjacent parts of Asia and North Africa. This is, however, not only a consequence of the fact that the Christian Church has not interfered with local custom in this part of the world. Close agnatic marriage is held to be an ideal in an area which, in spite of its marked economic diversity, shares many elements of a common culture. Within it, this type of marriage seems to be a logical outcome of two particular notions. The first is the conceptualisation of genealogical relations traced through men as constituting the closest links of kinship, and the second is the conceptualisation of men as responsible for the control of the conduct of women. Although neither of these notions is specifically Islamic in origin, both have, nevertheless, been reinforced by the Islamic tradition (for the relations between notions of honour and Islam see Dodd 1973).

The oft-quoted Koranic passages stating the greater importance of men than women (Koran 2: 228; 4: 34), and the well-known insistence on the inequality of men and women in matters of inheritance (4: 11), divorce (2: 272) and legal standing (2: 282), positively correlate with the emphasis on agnation and on tracing relations through men.

The conceptualisation of gender relations whereby men are charged with control of and responsibility for the conduct of women is, however, not traceable either to the Koran or *hadith*, which stress the spiritual, if not legal, equality of both sexes as well as the equal moral responsibility of men and women for their actions (Stowasser 1984: 20–3). It is rather the product of numerous exegeses of the Koranic text and *hadith* by mediaeval scholars and jurists (ibid.: 32–8), which have, in many respects, become more important than the Koran and *hadith* themselves in shaping the Islamic tradition. In this tradition, despite the Koranic injunction which puts men in charge of women, there is no belief in female inferiority, as Mernissi has forcibly argued: 'on the contrary, the whole system is based on the assumption that woman is a powerful and dangerous being. All sexual institutions (polygamy, repudiation, sexual segregation, etc.) can be perceived as a strategy for containing her power' (1975: xvi).

The woman's power derives from the fact that she is 'endowed with a fatal attraction which erodes the male's will to resist her and reduces him to a passive acquiescent role, whence her identification with *fitna*, chaos, and with the anti-divine and anti-social forces of the universe' (ibid.: 11; cf. Stowasser 1984: 32). Arabic writers pointed out that women have 'the power to deceive and defeat men, not by force, but by cunning and intrigue' (Mernissi 1975: 5); and, according to their interpretations, *hadith* is quite explicit about the fact that if women are not constrained, men face an irresistible sexual attraction which inevitably leads to *fitna* (ibid.: 11–12), distracting men from their social and religious duties. Imam al Ghazali sees civilisation as struggling to contain this destructive, all-absorbing power of women (ibid.: 4).

Mernissi has argued convincingly that Islam expects that the woman will not obey the divine order (ibid.: 40). The man's religious duty to control and discipline his female relatives, explicitly stated by Arab interpreters of the prophetic tradition (ibid.: 40), is the positive outcome of this expectation.

The two most important cultural notions which positively contribute to articulating the logic of agnatic in-marriage have been codified in Islamic tradition, and this accounts for the widely-held belief, often put forward by the natives themselves (cf. R. Tapper 1979: 141), that preference for FBD marriage has been enjoined by Islam.[3] The marriage of the Prophet's cousin 'Ali to the Prophet's daughter Fatima is often taken as an example of Islamic tradition to be followed by the faithful, and the preference for cousin marriage often follows the spread of Islam to Africa (Bates and Rassam 1983: 199; Lewis 1966: 52–3). But the notions about the pre-eminence of agnation over cognation and of men over women are part of a wider cultural tradition of which Islam has been just one specific articulation. This accounts, on the one hand, for the fact that preference for FBD marriage is expressed by many non-Muslims in the Middle East (Rosenfeld 1957; Goldberg 1967; Cresswell 1976) and, on the other hand, for the fact that, among some Muslims, FBD marriage is disapproved of or abhorred (Magnarella 1974: 87–90). Among others, no preference for it is expressed at all (Meeker 1976: 407–8) or, when expressed as an ideal, it is not followed in practice to any significant extent.[4]

FBD marriage and honour

Underlying this difference of attitude to FBD marriages are differences in the men's concern with their honour, which can be adversely affected by the conduct of women related to them in determinate ways. The anthropologists who have been concerned with analysing the preference for FBD marriage in its cultural context have emphasised the context of gender relations (Hilal 1972; Abu-Lughod 1986: 145 ff.) and, more specifically, have treated this type of marriage as an instrumental device employed in the strategy aimed at preserving men's honour (Antoun 1968: 693; Meeker 1976; Bourdieu 1977; Pitt-Rivers 1977: 161 ff.). Although men's honour cannot be accumulated or increased through the exemplary conduct of women under their control, it is adversely affected if women breach the code of modesty, and particularly if they become involved in illicit sexual acts. This renders men vulnerable, and dependent on the conduct of women under their control.

I would suggest that it is not the notion of honour as such that provides the key to the understanding of the meaning of the preference for in-marriage as opposed to out-marriage, but the notion of the common fund of honour, as yet another specific expression of the more general value of solidarity, and, in particular, the difference in the conceptualisation of whose honour is affected in the case of failure to control successfully the conduct of a *married* woman. Regrettably, most studies concerned with notions of honour and shame stress the fact that it is the responsibility of men to control the shame of their women and to defend their own honour through controlling the sexual conduct of their women, but they do not specify precisely which of the woman's male relatives are responsible for her conduct, or, particularly, to what extent this responsibility is transferred to her husband at marriage. Many ethnographies concerned with kinship and marriage in the Middle East, including those specifically concerned with expressed marriage preferences, do not give any account of the notions of honour and shame at all. As Dodd observes (1973: 42), this is probably due to the limitation of the ethnographic method rather than to the absence of these notions in the societies studied. Other studies treat the notions of honour and shame as if they were uniformly expressed throughout the Middle East, without paying any particular attention to their culturally-specific articulation in different Middle Eastern societies.[5]

From the studies which *have* paid adequate attention to these problems, it appears that in the non-Islamic cultures of the Mediterranean,[6] and in some Islamic cultures of the Middle East,[7] it is the husband's honour which is affected by the misconduct of his wife. Alternatively, a married woman's behaviour reflects on the honour both of her kinsmen and of her husband (Pastner 1972: 251, 256). In these systems, the woman is released from the control of the men of her own family upon marriage and becomes subject to the control of her husband, or her husband and his agnates (Stirling 1965: 161; N. Tapper 1981: 385, 394; N. and R. Tapper 1982: 164–5). The naming system whereby a woman adopts the name of her husband upon marriage[8] expresses symbolically the transfer of control from her father and brothers, whose name she bore before marriage, to her husband, whose name she now bears. The husband's genealogical relation to his wife is irrelevant: it is the marriage tie through which his own honour becomes affected. We are dealing here with a cultural system emphasising the solidarity of the family (Campbell 1965: 142; Stirling 1965: 174, 236) – which correlates positively with the relative emphasis on affinal as opposed to agnatic solidarity (R. Tapper 1979: 145–6) – or at lest with a system in which relations of affinity are clearly conceptualised as those of friendship and support (Stirling 1965: 172–3). (The Durrani of Afghanistan seem to be an exception (N. Tapper 1981: 394; N. and R. Tapper 1982: 162).) This, in its turn, correlates positively with the absence of the preference for FBD marriage (Meeker 1976: 407–8; N. Tapper 1981: 391), or with the fact that FBD marriage is disapproved of (Magnarella 1974: 87–90). It may possibly also correlate with only negligible occurrence of FBD marriage (which is still considered to be ideal) (Stirling 1965: 201–3; R. Tapper 1979: 140–4; Olesen 1982: 116); or the traditional right to marry the agnatic cousin is no longer enforced, or appears to be disappearing (Canfield 1973: 49–50). The lack of concern with hypergamy (Stirling 1965: 208; Meeker 1976: 392, n. 2; R. Tapper 1979: 144) is another characteristic feature of the societies of this type, but the Durrani seem again to be an exception (N. and R. Tapper 1982).[9]

In most Arabic and Islamic areas of the Middle East, it is the honour of the woman's agnates which is affected by her conduct, whether she is married or not.[10] They cannot release her from their control upon marriage, to protect their honour; and, culturally, she is indeed seen as permanently associated with her agnates. Among the Negev Bedouin, a ritual abduction of the bride takes place after the marriage arrangements have been completed and the marriage payment handed over. Morever, it is the bride's own group which insists on performing the capture, which

> indicates that it has given something beyond what it was morally entitled to; it has given a woman to another family or section, whereas a woman ideally remains all her life also a member of her group of origin ... The woman has been captured by force, as it were, and therefore she ought to be allowed to return to her father's tent (Marx 1967: 104).

J. Schneider (1971: 21) also sees bride capture and rivalry at the time of the wedding as symbolising the woman's continuous attachment to her father and brothers; and Ginat interprets similarly the fact that, among both Bedouin and rural Arabs in Israel, the members of the bride's family do not attend her wedding ceremony. He sees their non-attendance as symbolising 'that she has not left her home and that she continues to belong to her family of origin' (1987: 114–15).

Similar behaviour has occasionally been reported from other Middle Eastern societies. Among the Yomut Turkmen, for example, male agnates of the bride show little overt interest in the wedding celebration and are reserved in conduct. The bride should not be mentioned in their presence 'because of the "shame" they feel in association with a marriage of a close female agnate'. The women close to the groom have to remove the bride by force from her tent, the door of which has been barred by the women close to her (Irons 1975: 138). During marriage ceremonies among the Bedouin of Cyrenaica, 'the senior agnates stand aside and make a show of ignoring the proceedings' (Peters 1965: 131), and 'every effort is made to give substance to the expressed view that "nothing has happened"' (ibid.: 129).

That the responsibility for the woman's behaviour stays forever with her agnates, and is not transferred to her husband, is clearly indicated by the fact that the brother or father of a married woman is responsible for punishing her for improper behaviour (Barclay 1964: 108, 116; Abu-Lughod 1986: 55), and particularly by the fact that they, and not her husband, kill her if she commits adultery, in order to preserve their honour.[11] This seems also to be the case among the settlers on the Amik Plain (Aswad 1971: 54), although Aswad also reports a case of a man who shot his wife for alleged infidelity. She was, however, from an unrelated tribe which lived in a different region (ibid.). Webster reports for Morocco (though he may in fact be referring to a general Middle Eastern stereotype) that the husband is responsible for killing his wife's lover but the adulteress 'is killed by her father or brother, for it is their honour she has sullied' (1982: 180). Schneider generalises the situation in the following way:

An unmarried girl's loss of virginity brings unbearable shame to her family or lineage who, if they are to recover their honour, must first kill the girl and then her lover or seducer (this is the norm, although the form may deviate from it considerably). In patrilineal societies, responsibility for purification resides in brothers and first cousins, who remain the protectors of the women of the family even after these women marry. In cases of adultery, the husband (unless he is a parallel cousin) merely initiates divorce proceedings and tries to recover payments of bridewealth, while brothers and cousins go about avenging the honour of their family (J. Schneider 1971: 21).

The punishment is sometimes meted out not to the errant wife but to the adulterer. Among the Yörük of Turkey, 'it is the duty of the girl's brother, even in the case of married women, to secure family honour by punishing the transgressor' (Bates 1973: 69).

There is a conspicuous lack of information in the existing literature as to which rights in the woman are retained by her agnates and which are transferred to her husband and his group upon her marriage (see R. and N. Tapper 1988). There is, nevertheless, some indication of her continued incorporation in the agnatic line. For example, among the Bedouin of Cyrenaica, the father of a married woman, and not her husband, receives compensation for her killing, 'for a woman's "bone" always belongs to her father' (Peters 1967: 270). The same situation obtains among the Negev

Bedouin, from whom Marx reports a case of a father claiming compensation for the death caused to his daughter by her husband (1967: 237). Among the Rwala Bedouin, the agnates of a married woman bear the responsibility for bringing vengeance against her killer; and vengeance is directed towards them, and not towards her husband, if she herself committed murder (Musil 1928: 494). In a Tunisian village, a married woman is not incorporated into her husband's agnatic group but remains the responsibility of her father (Abu Zahra 1982: 85, 86). Her husband does not have the exclusive right to punish her, but she can still be beaten by her brother (ibid.: 89, 90). When she dies, her brothers or (in their absence) her brothers' sons are responsible for her burial, and the role of her husband's family is the same as that of any other villagers (ibid.: 87).

The continuous association of a married woman with her agnates is also indicated by the support she receives from them against her husband and his kin (Musil 1928: 239; Antoun 1972: 162; Abu-Lughod 1986: 54–5, 149). Her father or brothers may continue to support her and help her even against her husband, in spite of the fact that the rights which a father exercised over his daughter are formally transferred to her husband at marriage (Christensen 1982: 52). Christensen points out that among the Pakhtun in Kunar, 'the lack of support for a woman from her agnates does not necessarily derive from an absence of interest in her fate, but rather from the fact that their ability to assist her might be both limited and risky since marriages are either hypergamous or between social equals'. She is likely to enjoy continued support from her agnates, if for some reason, they are in a stronger position than those of her husband (ibid.: 59).

In some societies, a woman's agnates continue to control her property after her marriage (Cunnison 1966: 93). Divorced or widowed women often return to their agnates (Marx 1967: 185; Irons 1975: 147–8; Abu Zahra 1982: 87). Other ethnographers report norms, customs and institutions that also suggest the continuing attachment of a married woman to her agnates (Robertson Smith 1903: 77, 122, 125; Bates 1973: 39, 69, 101, 117; Lancaster 1981: 58–60).

The naming system whereby the woman retains the name of her father upon her marriage also clearly signifies her continued incorporation in her agnatic line. As the woman's behaviour does not reflect as much on her husband as on her agnates, there is no guarantee that the husband will properly control and protect his stranger-wife (Granqvist 1931: 94–5; Cohen 1965: 122). The situation is different if he himself is her agnate.

In his study of homicide for family honour among the Arabs in Israel, Kressel points out that the woman's conduct remains the concern of her family of origin even after her marriage, and that 'most muderers for family honour are agnates of their victim, often brothers, father, or father's brothers and their sons' (1981: 142–3). The husband's honour is, of course, affected through the conduct of his wife; but a man's jealousy does not justify her execution and, significantly, all the husbands accused of attacking their wives were also their agnates, with three out of four of them being their father's brother's sons (ibid.: 146). We are dealing here with a cultural system emphasising the solidarity of agnates, which correlates positively with the devaluation of conjugal relationships and affinity.

The cultural system which emphasises the solidarity of the family and the importance of affinal ties and that which emphasises the solidarity of agnates at the expense of conjugal relations are, of course, ideal types. They are, nevertheless, empirically realised in pure or almost pure form in quite a number of societies. On the other hand, there are societies which seem to combine in various degrees the features of both systems.

Of those to which have I paid specific attention in this essay, the Marri Baluch fall into this ambiguous category. They express a strong preference for marriages with patrilateral parallel cousins and other close agnates (Pehrson 1966: 57). The responsibility for the woman is transferred upon her marriage from her agnates to her husband. She is personally bound to him and he is said to 'own' her. No compensation is paid to anyone but him for damages caused to her and, if she commits murder, responsibility rests with him and not her agnates (ibid.: 42–3, 52–3). She is not, however, fully incorporated in her husband's group. There is no levirate (ibid.: 42, 53), and if her husband dies the rights over the widow revert to her agnates. Her remarriage is arranged by her closest agnate and the brideprice goes in full to her agnates. 'Emotionally, a woman always continues to identify herself with her natal group; the "home" of a married woman is her father's tent' (ibid.: 42–3). On the other hand, the duty to kill an unfaithful wife falls on the husband, or on his close agnates if he fails in his duty (ibid.: 41, 53). Even in this respect, however, the transfer of the responsibility for the woman's conduct to the husband and his group is not absolute: 'When a woman is discovered in adultery, and her husband's minimal lineage fails to exact punishment, the dormant interests of her natal group are recognised in her brother's – alternatively, father's – right to punish (ibid.: 43). It may well be that a married woman's behaviour affects the honour both of her agnates and of her husband. But is is equally possible that the clue to the 'dormant interest' of the woman's natal group lies in the fact that husbands are expected to be their wives' agnates, and most of them in fact are (Pehrson 1966: 57). The woman's father and brother may spring into action only when their honour has been sullied by their daughter's and sister's conduct and their agnate, to whom they entrusted her, has failed to act. As it is not at all clear from Pehrson's text to what extent the husband has a right and duty to kill his adulterous wife because he is her husband, and to what extent it is because he is her agnate, I do not think that the Marri Baluch ethnography can be taken as challenging my hypothesis without further research.

The same applies to the data on Swat Pukhtun, which indicate in a similar way the admixture of features characteristic of the two cultural systems. The woman's conduct affects the husband's honour (Barth 1959: 83; Lindholm 1982: 222) and he has the right to kill her if she misbehaves (Lindholm 1982: 219). According to Barth's report, she is released from the control of the men of her own family and becomes subject to the control of her husband (1959: 39). Relations of affinity are conceptualised as those of friendship and support, and this correlates positively with the absence of the preference for FBD marriage (ibid.: 40). According to Lindholm's report, the integration of women with husbands' groups is weak (1982: 145) and the woman remains closely associated with her patriline. Her honour derives from the position of her lineage, which she vehemently defends when it is insulted by her husband or members of his group. She looks to her own lineage for a sense of personal identity and pride as well as for help and support. The disgrace of her lineage is seen as her disgrace, and she stays forever loyal to her lineage brothers. If they are in need, she supports them with money which she may have stolen from her husband. Should she die without sons, any land she was given by her father reverts to her patriline. If a woman is killed, her own lineage and not that of her husband is responsible for revenge (ibid.: 126). Affinity is unimportant (ibid.: 149), and the relations with affines have the character of barely-concealed hostility (ibid.: 151); the concern with hypergamy is strongly expressed (ibid.: 145). FBD marriage is preferred alongside marriages with other cousins and, as among the Marri Baluch, most husbands are agnates of their wives (ibid.: 143–4). Again, to resolve the apparent ambiguity in the data, more information would be needed about the husband's rights over his wife, those which he holds in virtue of being a husband and those which may accrue to him because he is his wife's agnate.

The foregoing brief description of the two cultural systems encountered in the Middle East has outlined specific features of Middle Eastern cultures (or if these cultures are to be seen as discourse, certain themes in this discourse) which I consider to be the relevant context for the preference for patrilateral parallel cousin marriage. It has suggested that this preference relates to the system of gender relations in which men are charged with controlling the unharnessed female power, combined with undervaluation of affinal relationships at the expense of kinship ones, and with the conceptualisation of agnatic links as those of the closest – and in extreme cases the only – kinship. On the one hand, the preference for close agnatic marriages is a logical outcome of this system of notions; on the other hand, the preference itself contributes to the continuous production of this system. As it is not only the pragmatic advantages of particular marriages which the actors manipulate through their marriage strategies, but also their expressive aspects, the asserted preferences are an important factor in the decisions which underlie the actors' marriage strategies. These strategies, in their turn, constitute the key element in the continuous production of the logically-articulated system of the cultural meaning of gender relations, agnatic solidarity and marriage.

I fully realise that this conclusion may appear overgeneralised. This is to a great extent due to the lack of ethnographic data that would provide unambiguous answers to the specific questions raised in my discussion. I hope, nevertheless, that the questions I have raised – and to which I have often been able to give only tentative answers – will enable ethnographers to ask new questions in the field, and stimulate discussion on problems of the comparison of the constitutive elements of society and culture in various Middle Eastern settings.

Notes to Chapter 5

1 The most radical version of this explanation was formulated by Robertson Smith (1903), who suggested on the basis of philological and historical evidence that FBD marriage was a survival of the pre-Islamic rules of inheritance, according to which women themselves were treated as an inheritable property of the group, and the deceased's male kin had the right of the hand of his wife or daughter. This old rule was accommodated to later Koranic injunctions which prohibited the treatment of women as inheritable property, and a man's inheritance of his father's right to marry his FBD is the result of such accommodation (see also Chelhod 1964).

2 My usage of 'hypergamy' follows that of Parry (1979: 196) and 'refers to a norm which strongly recommends – but does not necessarily oblige – a man to marry his daughter to a groom of higher status. The minimum requirement of such systems is that a woman should preferably be married to a man of higher rank but may be married to an equal; and as a residual consequence of this, a man must necessarily marry an equal or inferior woman'.

3 For the relation between Islam and FBD marriage, see Khuri 1970: 598; Antoun 1976: 167–8.

4 Stirling 1965: 201; Pastner and Pastner 1972; R. Tapper 1979: 140–4; Lancaster 1981: 38, 61; Wikan 1982: 208.

5 Antoun 1968; Pierce 1971: 33–64; J. Schneider 1971; Black-Michaud 1975: 218–28; Peters 1980. For the formulation of two different cultural conceptualisations of honour and shame in the Middle East, see N. Tapper 1981: 405, n. 2; Van Sommers 1988: 115–19; and R. and N. Tapper 1988.

6 Pitt-Rivers 1954: 116; 1965: 46, 52; 1977: 23, 24, 29, 92; Campbell 1964: 152, 199; 1965: 146; Peristiany 1965b: 182.

7 Stirling 1965: 211; Canfield 1973: 38–9; Meeker 1976: 390; R. Tapper 1979: 128; N. and R. Tapper 1982: 165; Olesen 1982: 120.

8 Campbell 1964: 186; Denich 1974: 253; Magnarella 1974: 86; Pitt-Rivers 1977: 43,

49; Meeker 1976: 416; R. Tapper 1979: 122.

9   The ethnographic information on some societies is not detailed enough to indicate to what extent a woman is released from the control of her agnates upon marriage and becomes subject to the control of her husband. It seems that among the Basseri the interest in a married woman, and the exercise of control over her, may be shared between her kinsmen and her husband (Barth 1964: 34). As among other societies discussed here, the most important social unit is the individual family (ibid.: 11, 13, 15), and a high value is put on affinal relationships (ibid.: 32–6). Another similarity with the societies discussed here is the fact that no preference seems to be expressed for marriages with patrilateral parallel cousins (ibid.: 65), although marriages between kin occur frequently (ibid.: 35, 36).

10 Musil 1928: 239, 494; Dickson 1949: 115–16; Barclay 1964: 51–3; Bourdieu 1965: 223; Abou-Zeid 1965: 257; Marx 1967: 104; Khuri 1970: 605–6; Aswad 1971: 54; Dodd 1973: 44–5; Cohen 1965: 122; 1974: 116; Black-Michaud 1975: 221; Abu-Lughod 1986: 158–9; see also Lewis 1965: 103–4.

11 Dickson 1949: 115, 144; Salim 1962: 58, 61; Abou-Zeid 1965: 253, 254, 257; Khuri 1970: 606; Bates 1973: 69; Cohen 1965: 122; 1974: 116; Irons 1975: 98, 102, but see also 103–4; Kressel 1981: 143, quoting Rosenfeld; Ginat 1987: 116. Fuller mentions that in a Muslim Lebanese village an adulterous woman theoretically deserves to be killed by her husband (1961: 69), but this appears exceptional to the area. Her account is probably more accurate when she adds that in practice 'a married woman who is believed to be, or is caught in the act of, carrying on clandestine relations is severely beaten by her husband or is divorced by him' (ibid.: 69). Such practice would be predictable from the rest of her ethnography, which suggests a continuous association of the married woman with her agnates (ibid.: 62).

References

Abercrombie, N., S. Hill and B. S. Turner. 1980. *The dominant ideology thesis*. London: Allen & Unwin.
Abou-Zeid, A. A. M. 1965. Honour and shame among the Bedouin of Egypt. In J. G. Peristiany (ed.), *Honour and shame: the values of Mediterranean society*: 243–59. London: Weidenfeld & Nicolson.
Abu-Lughod, L. 1986. *Veiled sentiments: honor and poetry in a Bedouin society*. Berkeley and Los Angeles: University of California Press.
Abu Zahra, N. 1976. Family and kinship in a Tunisian peasant community. In J. G. Peristiany (ed.), *Mediterranean family structures*: 157–71. Cambridge: Cambridge University Press.
— 1982. *Sidi Ameur: a Tunisian village*. London: Ithaca Press.
Anderson, J. W. 1982. Cousin marriage in context: constructing social relations in Afghanistan. *Folk* 24: 7–28.
Antoun, R. T. 1968. On the modesty of women in Arab Muslim villages: a study in the accommodation of traditions. *American Anthropologist* 70: 671–97.
— 1972. *Arab village: a social structural study of trans-Jordanian peasant community*. Bloomington: Indiana University Press. (Quoted from 1977 edition.)
— 1976. Anthropology. In L. Binder (ed.), *The study of the Middle East*: 137–228. New York: John Wiley & Sons.
Ardener, E. 1971. The new anthropology and its critics. *Man* (NS) 6: 449–67.
Asad, T. 1970. *The Kababish Arabs: power, authority and consent in a nomadic tribe*. London: C. Hurst.
— 1986. The concept of cultural translation in British social anthropology. In J. Clifford and G. E. Marcus (eds), *Writing culture: the poetics and politics of ethnography*: 141–64, Berkeley: University of California Press.
Aswad, B. C. 1971. *Property control and social strategies: settlers on a Middle Eastern plain* (Anthropological Papers of the Museum of Anthropology, University of Michigan, 44). Ann Arbor: The University of Michigan.
Ayoub, M. 1959. Parallel cousin marriage and endogamy: a study in sociometry. *Southwestern Journal of Anthropology* 15: 266–75.
Baer, G. 1964. *Population and society in the Arab East*. New York: Praeger.

Barclay, H. B. 1964. *Buuri al Lamaab: a suburban village in the Sudan.* Ithaca, NY: Cornell University Press.
Barnard, A. and A. Good. 1984. *Research practices in the study of kinship* (ASA Research Methods in Social anthropology 2). London: Academic Press.
Barnes, R. H. 1985. Hierarchy without caste. In R. H. Barnes, D. de Coppet and R. J. Parkin (eds), *Contexts and levels: anthropological essays on hierarchy* (JASO Occasional Papers 4): 8–20. Oxford: JASO.
Barth, F. 1953. *Principles of social organization in southern Kurdistan* (Universitetets Etnografiske Museum Bulletin 7). Oslo: Brødrene Jørgensen A/S.
— 1954. Father's brother's daughter marriage in Kurdistan. *Southwestern Journal of Anthropology* 10: 164–71.
— 1959. *Political leadership among Swat Pathans.* London: Athlone Press.
— 1964. *Nomads of South Persia: the Basseri tribe of the Khamseh confederacy.* London: Allen & Unwin.
— 1973. Descent and marriage reconsidered. In J. Goody (ed.), *The character of kinship:* 3–19. Cambridge: Cambridge University Press.
Bates, D. G. 1973. *Nomads and farmers: a study of the Yörük of southeastern Turkey* (Anthropological Papers of the Museum of Anthropology, University of Michigan, 52). Ann Arbor: University of Michigan.
— 1974. Normative and alternative systems of marriage among the Yörük of southeastern Turkey. *Anthropological Quarterly* 47: 270–87.
Bates, D. and A. Rassam. 1983. *Peoples and cultures of the Middle East.* Englewood Cliffs, NJ: Prentice-Hall.
Beattie, J. 1964. *Other cultures: aims, methods and achievements in social anthropology.* London: Cohen & West.
Black-Michaud, J. 1975. *Cohesive force: feud in the Mediterranean and the Middle East.* Oxford: Basil Blackwell.
Bois, T. 1966. *The Kurds.* Beirut: Khayats.
Bourdieu, P. 1965. The sentiment of honour in Kabyle society. In J. G. Peristiany (ed.), *Honour and shame: the values of Mediterranean society:* 191–241. London: Weidenfeld & Nicolson.
— 1977. *Outline of a theory of practice.* Cambridge: Cambridge University Press.
Bradburd, D. 1984. The rules of the game: the practice of marriage among the Komachi. *American Ethnologist* 11: 738–53.
Campbell, J. K. 1964. *Honour, family and patronage.* London: Oxford University Press. (Quoted from 1974 edition.)
— 1965. Honour and the devil. In J. G. Peristiany (ed.), *Honour and shame: the values of a Mediterranean society:* 141–70. London: Weidenfeld & Nicolson.
Canfield, R. L. 1973. *Faction and conversion in a plural society: religious alignments in the Hindu Kush* (Anthropological Papers of the Museum of Anthropology, University of Michigan, 50). Ann Arbor: The University of Michigan.
Chatila, K. 1934. *Le mariage chez les musulmans en Syrie.* Paris.
Chelhod, J. 1964. Le mariage avec la cousine parallèle dans le système arabe. *L'Homme* 4: 113–73.
Christensen, A. 1982. Agnates, affines and allies: patterns of marriage among Pakhtun in Kunar, north-east Afghanistan. *Folk* 24: 29–63.

References

Cohen, A. 1965. *Arab border-villages in Israel: a study of continuity and change in social organization.* Manchester: Manchester University Press.
— 1974. *Two-dimensional man: an essay on the anthropology of power and symbolism in complex society.* London: Routledge & Kegan Paul.
Cole, D. P. 1973. The enmeshment of nomads in Sa'udi Arabian society: the case of Āl Murrah. In C. Nelson (ed.), *The desert and the sown: nomads in the wider society* (Institute of International Studies Research Series 21). Berkeley: University of California.
— 1975. *Nomads of the nomads: the Āl Murrah Bedouin of the Empty Quarter.* Arlington Heights, Ill.: AHM.
— 1984. Alliance and descent in the Middle East and the 'problem' of patrilateral parallel cousin marriage. In A. S. Ahmed and D. M. Hart (eds), *Islam in tribal societies: from the Atlas to the Indus: 169–86.* London: Routledge & Kegan Paul.
Comaroff, J. L. 1980. Introduction to J. L. Comaroff (ed.), *The meaning of marriage payments:* 1–47. London: Academic Press.
Comaroff, J. L. and J. Comaroff. 1981. The management of marriage in a Tswana chiefdom. In E. J. Krige and J. L. Comaroff (eds), *Essays on African marriage in Southern Africa:* 29–49. Johannesburg: Juta.
Coon, C. 1958. *Caravan: the story of the Middle East.* New York: Holt, Rinehart & Winston.
Gresswell, R. 1976. Lineage endogamy among maronite mountaineers. In J. G. Peristiany (ed.), *Mediterranean family structures:* 101–14. Cambridge: Cambridge University Press.
Crick, M. 1976. *Explorations in language and meaning: towards a semantic anthropology.* London: Malaby Press.
— 1985. 'Tracing' the anthropological self: quizzical reflections on fieldwork, tourism, and the ludic. *Social Analysis* 17: 71–92.
Cuisenier, J. 1962. Endogamie et exogamie dans le mariage arabe. *L'Homme* 2: 80–105.
Cunnison, I. 1966. *Baggara Arabs: power and the lineage in a Sudanese nomad tribe.* Oxford: Clarendon Press.
Davies, R. P. 1949. Syrian Arabic kinship terms. *Southwestern Journal of Anthropology* 5: 244–2.
Davis, J. 1977. *People of the Mediterranean: an essay in comparative social anthropology.* London: Routledge & Kegan Paul.
Denich, B. S. 1974. Sex and power in the Balkans. In M. Z. Rosaldo and L. Lamphere (eds), *Woman, culture and society:* 243–62. Standford: Standford University Press.
Dickson, H. R. P. 1949. *The Arab of the desert: a glimpse into Badawin life in Kuwait and Sau'di Arabia.* London: Allen & Unwin.
Dodd, P. C. 1973. Family honor and the forces of change in Arab society. *International Journal of Middle Studies* 4: 40–54.
Donnan, H. 1985. The rules and rhetoric of marriage negotiations among the Dhund Abbasi of northern Pakistan. *Ethnology* 24: 183–96.
Eickelman, D. F. 1976. *Moroccan Islam: tradition and society in a pilgrimage center.* Austin: University of Texas Press.
— 1981. *The Middle East: an anthropological approach.* Englewood Cliffs, NJ:

Prentice-Hall.
Ferdinand, K. 1982. Marriage among Pakhtun nomads of eastern Afghanistan. *Folk* 24: 65–87.
Fernea, R. A. and J. M. Malarkey. 1975. Anthropology of the Middle East and North Africa: a critical assessment. *Annual Review of Anthropology* 4: 183–206.
Fischer, M. M. J. 1978. On changing the concept and position of Persian women. In L. Beck and N. Keddie (eds), *Women in the Muslim world:* 189–215. Harvard: Harvard University Press.
Fodor, J. A. 1975. *The language of thought.* New York: Cromwell.
Fortes, M. 1953. The structure of unilineal descent groups. *American Anthropologist* 55: 17–41.
Fuller, A. H. 1961. *Buarij: portrait of a Lebanese Muslim village* (Harvard Middle Eastern Monographs 6). Cambridge, Mass.: Harvard University Press.
Geertz, H. 1979. The meaning of family ties. In C. Geertz, H. Geertz, and L. Rosen, *Meaning and order in Moroccan society: the essay in cultural analysis:* 315–91. Cambridge: Cambridge University Press.
Gellner, E. 1969. *Saints of the Atlas.* London: Weidenfeld & Nicolson.
— 1970. Concepts and society. In B. R. Wilson (ed.), *Rationality:* 18–49. Oxford: Basil Blackwell.
— 1973a. The new idealism: cause and meaning in the social sciences. In I. C. Jarvie and J. Agassi (eds), *Cause and meaning in the social sciences:* 50–76. London: Routledge & Kegan Paul.
— 1873b. Time and theory in social anthropology. In I. C. Jarvie and J. Agassi (eds), *Cause and meaning in the social sciences:* 88–106. London: Routledge & Kegan Paul.
Gilbert, J. P. and E. A. Hammel. 1966. Computer simulation and analysis of problems in kinship and social structure. *American Anthropologist* 68: 71–93.
Ginat, J. 1987. *Blood disputes among Bedouin and rural Arabs in Israel: revenge, mediation, outcasting and family honor.* Pittsburgh: University of Pittsburgh Press.
Gluckman, M. 1956. *Custom and conflict in Africa.* Oxford: Basil Blackwell.
Goldberg, H. 1967. FBD marriage and demography among Tripolitanian Jews in Israel. *Southwestern Journal of Anthropology* 23: 177–91.
Goody, J. 1973. Bridewealth and dowry in Africa and Eurasia. In J. Goody and S. J. Tambiah, *Bridewealth and dowry* (Cambridge Papers in Social Anthropology 7): 1–58. Cambridge: Cambridge University Press.
— 1976. *Production and reproduction: a comparative study of the domestic domain.* Cambridge: Cambridge University Press.
— 1983. *The development of the family and marriage in Europe.* Cambridge: Cambridge University Press.
Granqvist, H. 1931. *Marriage conditions in a Palestinian village.* Commentationes Humanarum Literarum III 8. Helsingfors: Societas Scientiarium Fennica.
Guichard, P. 1977. *Structures sociales 'orientales' et 'occidentales' dans l'Espagne musulmane.* Paris: Mouton.
Gulick, J. 1955. *Social structure and culture change in a Lebanese village* (Viking Fund Publications in Anthropology 21). New York: Wenner-Gren Foundation for Anthropological Research.

References

— 1976. *The Middle East: and anthropological perspective*. Pacific Palisades, Calif.: Goodyear.
Hammel, E. A. and H. Goldberg. 1971. Parallel cousin marriage. *Man* (NS) 3: 488–9.
Heath, A. 1976. *Rational choice and social exchange: a critique of exchange theory*. Cambridge: Cambridge University Press.
Hilal, J. M. 1972. Father's brother's daughter marriage in Arab communities: a problem for sociological explanation. *Middle East Forum* 46: 73–84.
Hobart, M. 1982. Meaning or moaning?: an ethnographic note on a little-understood tribe. In D. Parkin (ed.), *Semantic anthropology* (ASA Monographs 22): 39–63. London: Academic Press.
— 1985. Texte est un con. In R. H. Barnes, D. de Coppet and R. J. Parkin (eds), *Contexts and levels: anthropological essays on hierarchy*: 33–53. Oxford: JASO.
— 1986. Introduction: context, meaning, and power. In M. Hobart and R. H. Taylor (eds), *Context, meaning and power in Southeast Asia*: 7–19. Ithaca, NY: Cornell University Press.
Holy, L. 1974. *Neighbours and kinsmen: a study of the Berti people of Darfur*. London: C. Hurst.
Holy, L. and M. Stuchlik. 1983. *Actions, norms and representations: foundations of anthropological inquiry*. Cambridge: Cambridge University Press.
Homans, G. C. and D. M. Schneider. 1955. *Marriage, authority, and final causes: a study of unilateral cross-cousin marriage*. Glencoe, Ill.: Free Press.
Hopkins, K. 1980. Brother-sister marriage in Roman Egypt. *Comparative Studies in Society and History* 22: 303–54.
Irons, W. 1975. *The Yomut Turkmen: a study of social organization among a Central Asian Turkic-speaking population* (Anthropological Papers of the Museum of Anthropology, University of Michigan, 58). Ann Arbor: The University of Michigan.
Kaplan, J. O. 1973. Endogamy and the marriage alliance: a note on continuity in kindred-based groups. *Man* (NS) 8: 55–70.
Keesing, R. M. 1970. Toward a model of role analysis. In R. Naroll and R. Cohen (eds), *A handbook of method in cultural anthropology*: 423–53. New York: Columbia University Press.
— 1972. Simple models of complexity: the lure of kinship. In P. Reining (ed.), *Kinship studies in the Morgan centennial year*: 17–31. Washington, DC: The Anthropological Society of Washington.
Keyser, J. M. B. 1974. The Middle Eastern Case: is there a marriage rule? *Ethnology* 13: 293–309.
Khuri, F. I. 1970. Parallel cousin marriage reconsidered: a Middle Eastern practice that nullifies the effects of marriage on the intensity of family relationships. *Man* (NS) 5: 597–618.
Kressel, G. 1981. Sororicide/filiacide: homicide for family honour. *Current Anthropology* 22: 141–58.
— 1986. Prescriptive patrilateral parallel cousin marriage: the perspective of the bride's father and brothers. *Ethnology* 25: 163–80.
Lancaster, W. 1981. *The Rwala Bedouin today*. Cambridge: Cambridge University Press.

Larson, B. K. 1983. Tunisian kin ties reconsidered. *American Ethnologist* 10: 551–70.
Leach, E. R. 1960. The Sinhalese of the dry zone of northern Ceylon. In G. P. Murdock (ed.), *Social structure in Southeast Asia* (Viking Fund Publications in Anthropology 29): 116–26. New York: Wenner-Gren Foundation for Anthropological Research.
Leech, G. 1981. *Semantics: the study of meaning.* 2nd ed. London: Penguin.
Lévi-Strauss, C. 1969. *The elementary structures of kinship.* London: Eyre & Spottiswoode.
Lewis, I. M. 1965. Problems in the comparative study of unilineal descent. In M. Banton (ed.), *The relevance of models for social anthropology* (ASA Monographs 1): 87–112. London: Tavistock.
— 1966. *Islam in tropical Africa.* London: Oxford University Press for the International African Institute.
Lindholm, C. 1982. *Generosity and jealousy: the Swat Pakhtun of northern Pakistan.* New York: Columbia University Press.
Lutfiyya, A. M. 1966. *Baytin, a Jordanian village: a study of social institutions and social change in a folk community.* The Hague: Mouton.
Luzbetak, L. 1951. *Marriage and family in Caucasia.* Studia Instituti Anthropos 3. Wien-Mödlingen: St Gabriel's Mission Press.
Lyons, J. 1981. *Language, meaning and context.* London: Fontana Paperbacks.
McCabe, J. 1983. FBD marriage: further support for the Westermarck hypothesis of the incest taboo? *American Anthropologist* 85: 50–69.
Magnarella, P. J. 1974. *Tradition and change in a Turkish town.* New York: John Wiley & Sons.
Maher, V. 1974. *Women and property in Morocco: their changing relation to the process of social stratification in the Middle Atlas.* Cambridge: Cambridge University Press.
Marx, E. 1967. *Bedouin of the Negev.* Manchester: Manchester University Press.
Meeker, M. E. 1976. Meaning and society in the Near East: examples from the Black Sea Turks and the Levantine Arabs. *International Journal of Middle East Studies* 7: 243–70, 383–422.
Mernissi, F. 1975. *Beyond the veil: male–female dynamics in a modern Muslim society.* New York: John Wiley & Sons.
Milton, K. 1982. Meaning and context: the interpretation of greetings in Kasigau. In D. Parkin (ed.), *Semantic anthropology* (ASA Monographs 22): 261–77. London: Academic Press.
Murphy, R. F. 1971. *The dialectics of social life: alarms and excursions in anthropological theory.* London: Allen & Unwin.
Murphy, R. F. and L. Kasdan. 1959. The structure of parallel cousin marriage. *American Anthropologist* 61: 17–29.
— 1967. Agnation and endogamy: some further considerations. *Southwestern Journal of Anthropology* 23: 1–14.
Musil, A. 1928. *The manners and customs of the Rwala Bedouins.* New York: Crane.
Nassehi-Behnam, V. 1985. Change and the Iranian family. *Current Anthropology* 26: 557–62.

Needham, R. 1958. A structural analysis of Purum society. *American Anthropologist* 60: 75–101.
— 1971. Remarks on the analysis of kinship and marriage. In R. Needham (ed.), *Rethinking kinship and marriage* (ASA Monographs 11): 1–34 London: Tavistock.
Olesen, A. 1982. Marriage norms and practices in a rural community in North Afghanistan. *Folk* 24: 11–41.
Ortner, S. B. and H. Whitehead. 1981. Accounting for sexual meanings. Introduction to S. B. Ortner and H. Whitehead (eds), *Sexual meanings: the cultural construction of gender and sexuality:* 1–27. Cambridge: Cambridge University Press.
Parkin, D. 1982. Introduction to D. Parkin (ed.), *Semantic anthropology* (ASA Monographs 22): xi–li. London: Academic Press.
Parry, J. P. 1979. *Caste and kinship in Kangra.* London: Routledge & Kegan Paul.
Pastner, C. McC. 1972. A social, structural and historical analysis of honor, shame and purdah. *Anthropological Quarterly* 45: 248–61.
— 1979. Cousin marriage among the Zikri Baluch of coastal Pakistan. *Ethnology* 18: 31–47.
— 1981. The negotiation of bilateral endogamy in the Middle Eastern context: the Zikri Baluch example. *Journal of Anthropological Research* 37: 305–18.
— 1986. The Westermarck hypothesis and first cousin marriage: the cultural modification of negative sexual imprinting. *Journal of Anthropological Research* 42: 572–86.
Pastner, S. and C. McC. Pastner. 1972. Agriculture, kinship and politics in southern Baluchistan. *Man* (NS) 7: 128–36.
Patai, R. 1955. Cousin-right in Middle Eastern marriage. *Southwestern Journal of Anthropology* 11: 371–90.
— 1962. *Golden river to golden road: society, culture and change in the Middle East.* Philadelphia: University of Pennsylvania Press.
— 1965. The structure of endogamous unilineal descent groups. *Southwestern Journal of Anthropology* 21: 325–50.
Pehrson, R. N. 1966. *The social organization of the Marri Baluch* (Viking Fund Publications in Anthropology 43). New York: Wenner-Gren Foundation for Anthropological Research.
Peristiany, J. G. (ed.). 1965a. *Honour and shame: the values of Mediterranean society.* London: Weidenfeld & Nicolson.
— 1965b. Honour and shame in a Cypriot highland village. In J. G. Peristiany (ed.), *Honour and shame: the values of Mediterranean society:* 171–90. London: Weidenfeld & Nicolson.
Peters, E. L. 1960. The proliferation of segments in the lineage of the Bedouin of Cyrenaica. *Journal of the Royal Anthropological Institute* 90: 29–53.
— 1963. Aspects of rank and status among Muslims in a Lebanese village. In J. Pitt-Rivers (ed.), *Mediterranean countrymen:* 159–200. Paris: Mouton.
— 1965. Aspects of the family among the Bedouin of Cyrenaica. In M. F. Nimkoff (ed.), *Comparative family systems:* 121–64. Boston: Houghton Mifflin.
— 1967. Some structural aspects of the feud among the camel-herding Bedouin of Cyrenaica. *Africa* 37: 261–82.

— 1976. Aspects of affinity in a Lebanese Maronite village. In J. G. Peristiany (ed.), *Mediterranean family structures:* 27–79. Cambridge: Cambridge University Press.
— 1980. Aspects of Bedouin bridewealth among camel herders in Cyrenaica. In J. L. Comaroff (ed.), *The meaning of marriage payments:* 125–60. London: Academic Press.
Pierce, J. E. 1971. *Understanding the Middle East.* Rutland, Vermont: Charles E. Tuttle.
Ritt-Rivers, J. 1954. *The people of the Sierra.* London: Weidenfeld & Nicolson.
— 1965. Honour and social status. In J. G. Peristiany (ed.), *Honour and shame: the values of Mediterranean society:* 19–77. London: Weidenfeld & Nicolson.
— 1977. *The fate of Schechem or the politics of sex: essays in the anthropology of the Mediterranean.* Cambridge: Cambridge University Press.
Pocock, D. F. 1971. *Social anthropology.* 2nd ed. London: Sheed & Ward.
Randolph, R. and A. D. Coult, 1968. A computer analysis of Bedouin marriage. *Southwestern Journal of Anthropology* 24: 83–99.
Rivière, P. G. 1971. Marriage: a reassessment. In R. Needham (ed.), *Rethinking kinship and marriage* (ASA Monographs 11): 57–74. London: Tavistock.
Robertson Smith, W. 1903. *Kinship and marriage in early Arabia.* London: A. & C. Black.
Rosen, L. 1972. Muslim–Jewish relations in a Moroccan city. *International Journal of Middle East Studies* 3: 435–9.
— 1984. *Bargaining for reality: the construction of social relations in a Muslim community.* Chicago: University of Chicago Press.
Rosenfeld, H. 1957. An analysis of marriage and marriage statistics for a Moslem and Christian Arab village. *International Archives of Ethnography* 48: 32–62.
— 1958. Process of structural change within the Arab village extended family. *American Anthropologist* 60: 1127–39.
— 1968. The contradictions between property, kinship and power, as reflected in the marriage system of an Arab village. In J. G. Peristiany (ed.), *Contributions to Mediterranean sociology:* 247–60. Paris: Mouton.
— 1976. Social and economic factors in explanation of the increased rate of patrilineal endogamy in the Arab village in Israel. In J. G. Peristiany (ed.), *Mediterranean family structures:* 115–36. Cambridge: Cambridge University Press.
Sahlins, M. 1976. *Culture and practical reason.* Chicago: University of Chicago Press.
Salim, S. M. 1962. *Marsh dwellers of the Euphrates delta.* London School of Economics Monographs on Social Anthropology 23. London: Athlone Press.
Sampson, G. 1980. *Making sense.* London: Oxford University Press.
Schapera, I. 1950. Kinship and marriage among the Tswana. In A. R. Radcliffe-Brown and D. Forde (eds), *African systems of kinship and marriage:* 140–65. London: Oxford University Press.
— 1957. Marriage of near kin among the Tswana. *Africa* 27: 139–59.
— 1963. Agnatic marriage in Tswana royal families. In I. Schapera (ed.), *Studies in kinship and marriage* (Royal Anthropological Institute Occasional Papers 16). London.

Scheffler, H. W. 1966. Ancestor worship in anthropology: or, observation on descent and descrnt groups. *Current Anthropology* 1966: 541–51.
Schneider, D. M. 1976. Notes toward a theory of culture. In K. H. Basso and H. A. Selby (eds), *Meaning in anthropology:* 197–220. Albuquerque: University of New Mexico Press.
Schneider, J. 1971. Of vigilance and virgins: honor, shame and access to resources in Mediterranean societies. *Ethnology* 10: 1–24.
Skorupski, J. 1976. *Symbol and theory: a philosophical study of theories of religion in social anthropology.* Cambridge: Cambridge University Press.
Sperber, D. 1982. Apparently irrational beliefs. In M. Hollis and S. Lukes (eds), *Rationality and relativism:* 149–80. Oxford: Basil Blackwell.
Stirling, P. 1965. *Turkish village.* London: Weidenfeld & Nicolson.
Stowasser, B. F. 1984. The status of women in early Islam. In F. Hussain (ed.), *Muslim women:* 11–42. London: Croom Helm.
Strathern, M. 1987. Out of context: the persuasive fictions of anthropology. *Current Anthropology* 28: 251–81.
Stuchlik, M. 1976. Whose knowledge? In L. Holy (ed.), *Knowledge and behaviour.* The Queens University Papers in Social Anthropology 1: 1–25. Belfast: The Queen's University.
Tambiah, S. J. 1973. Dowry and bridewealth and the property rights of women in South Asia. In J. Goody and S. Tambiah, *Bridewealth and dowry* (Cambridge Papers in Social Anthropology 7): 59–169. Cambridge: Cambridge University Press.
Tapper, N. 1981. Direct exchange and brideprice: alternative forms in a complex marriage system. *Man* (NS) 16: 387–407.
Tapper, N. and R. Tapper. 1982. Marriage preferences and ethnic relations among Durrani Pashtuns of Afghan Turkestan. *Folk* 24: 157–77.
Tapper, R. 1979. *Pasture and politics: economics, conflict and ritual among Shahsevan nomads of northwestern Iran.* London: Academic Press.
Tapper, R. and N. Tapper. 1988. Marriage, honour and responsibility: Islamic and local models in the Mediterranean and the Middle East. Paper presented to the workshop on Islam Family Law in Theory and Practice. Cambridge, January 1988.
Tillion, G. 1983. *The republic of cousins: women's oppression in Mediterranean society:* London: Al Seqi.
Tyler, S. 1978. *The said and the unsaid.* London: Academic Press.
Uberoi, J. P. Singh. 1971. Men, women and property in northern Afghanistan. In S. T. Lokhandwalla (ed.), *India and contemporary Islam.* Simla: Indian Institute of Advanced Study.
Van Sommers, P. 1988. *Jealousy: what is it and who feels it?* London: Penguin.
Verdon, M. 1981. Agnatic descent and endogamy: a note, *Journal of Anthropological Research* 37: 247–55.
Webster, S. K. 1982. Women, sex and marriage in Moroccan proverbs. *International Journal of Middle East Studies* 14: 173–84.
Wellhausen, J. 1893. Die Ehe bei den Arabern. *Nachrichten von der Königlichen Gesellschaft der Wissenschaften und der Georg-Augusts-Universität zu Göttingen* 11: 431–81.
Westermarck, E. 1891. *The history of human marriage.* London: Macmillan.

Wikan, U. 1982. *Behind the veil in Arabia: women in Oman.* Baltimore: Johns Hopkins University Press.
Youssef, N. H. 1978. The status and fertility patterns of Muslim women. In L. Beck and N. Keddie (eds), *Women in the Muslim world:* 69–99. Cambridge, Mass.: Harvard University Press.

Index

Abercrombie, N. S., 36
Abou-Zeid, A. A. M., 14 n. 2, 128 n. 10, n. 11
Abu-Lughod, L., 14 n. 2, 26, 43 n. 3, 70 n. 1, 91 n. 6, 120, 123, 124, 128 n. 10
Abu-Zahra, N., 14 n. 2, 41, 140 n. 6, 118, 124
adultery, 29, 123, 125, 128 n. 11
affinity, 2, 28, 46, 56, 58–9, 78–86, 89, 91 n. 5, n. 6, 98, 111, 117–18, 122, 125–6, 128 n. 9
Afghanistan, 94, 122
Africa 17, 120
agnatic solidarity, 54, 76, 80, 83–4, 87, 93, 98, 102, 111–14, 116, 118, 122, 125, 127
alliance, 12, 43 n. 2, 46, 79, 101, 117, 118
Āl Murrah, 19, 30–2, 34, 44 n. 4, 78–80, 91 n. 5
Amik Plain, 87, 90, 91 n. 3, 123
analytical meaning, 19, 39–40, 111
analytical practice, 10, 15–17, 114
Anderson, J. W., 4, 33, 70 n. 2, 91 n. 1, 104 n. 2
Antoun, R. T., 19, 20, 43 n. 3, n. 4, 48, 95, 121, 124, 127 n. 3, n. 5
Arabia, 19, 78
Arabs, 16, 83, 85, 95, 118, 122, 124
Ardener, E., 36
Asad, T., 43 n. 3, 96–100, 104 n. 2, 108, 109
assumptions about explanation, 3, 7, 8

Aswad, B. C., 87–8, 91 n. 3, 104 n. 3, 123, 128 n. 10
Awlad 'Ali, 26, 70 n. 1
Ayoub, M., 5, 6, 17–18, 21

Baer, G., 62
Baggara, 19, 29–32, 34–5
Barclay, H. B., 43 n. 5, 85, 95, 104 n. 2, 123, 128 n. 10
Barnard, A. 4, 43 n. 2
Barnes, R. H., 36
Barth, F., 5, 14 n. 2, 17, 31–2, 43 n. 5, 44 n. 10, 46, 62–3, 77–8, 85, 91 n. 3, 94, 104 n. 2, 116, 126, 128 n. 9
Basseri, 128 n. 9
Bates, D. G., 14 n. 2, 20, 43 n. 5, n. 8, 74, 92 n. 9, 104 n. 1, 120, 123, 124, 128 n. 11
Beattie, J., 115
Bedouin, 16, 19, 22, 26, 30, 34, 70 n. 1, 77–9, 86–90, 91 n. 5, 122–4
Berti, 13, 14 n. 7, 23–8, 30–2, 34–5, 48–61, 64–7, 72–5, 110, 116, 118
Black-Michaud, J. 127 n. 5, 128 n. 10
Bois, T., 14 n. 2
Bourdieu, P., 4, 15, 26, 41, 44 n. 8, 58, 62, 67, 70 n. 4, 90 n. 1, 91 n. 6, 93, 100, 104 n. 2, n. 6, 110, 121, 128 n. 10
Bradburd, D., 10, 34, 43 n. 5
bridewealth, 63–5, 77–8, 102–3, 125

Campbell, J. K., 122, 127 n. 6, n. 8

Canfield, R. L., 122, 127 n. 7
causes, 10, 83, 106
Central Asia, 14 n. 1
Chatila, K., 62
Chelhod, J., 43 n. 2, 104 n. 2, n. 3
Christensen, A., 92 n. 9, 94, 104 n. 3, n. 6, 124
classification of marriages, 23, 30–3, 42, 54, 87
Cohen, A., 4, 19, 20, 80–4, 95–6, 103 n. 1, 104 n. 2, n. 3, n. 6, 118, 124, 128 n. 10, n. 11
Cole, D. P., 20, 30, 43 n. 4, 44 n. 9, 78–80, 91 n. 5, 104 n. 6, 118
Comaroff, J., 91 n. 4
Comaroff, J. L., 36–7, 91 n. 4
computer simulation, 18, 34
conceptualisation of kinship, 23–30, 33, 42
conceptual representation, 61
context definition, 63, 107, 109–10
contextualisation, 10, 11, 105–6, 108–10, 114
Coon, C., 118
Coult, A. D., 25, 34–5, 43 n. 5, 44 n. 8, 104 n. 6
Cresswell, R., 95, 104 n. 2, 120
Crick, M., 5, 36, 106, 107
cross-cousin marriage, 19, 21–2, 26, 29, 30, 33, 59–61
Cuisenier, J., 43 n. 2
cultural form, 5, 47
cultural meaning, 13, 15, 32, 39–42, 62, 93, 111, 127
Cunnison, I., 14 n. 2, 20, 29–30, 43 n. 3, 124
Cyrenaica, 16, 123

Davies, R. P., 43 n. 4
Davis, J., 4
decontextualisation, 37
demography, 12, 117, 118
Denich, B. S., 127 n. 8
Dhund, 9, 10, 34
Dickson, H. R. P., 14 n. 2, 128 n. 10, n. 11
discourse, 4, 14 n. 5, 126
divorce, 119, 124

diya, 58, 76, 91 n. 2
Dodd, P. C., 119, 121, 128 n. 10
Donnan, H., 9, 10, 34
dowry, 64
Druze, 21
Durrani, 122

Egypt, 26, 70 n. 1
Eickelman, D. F., 41, 43 n. 7, 48, 110
endogamy, 6, 12, 16–23, 27, 43 n. 1, 82, 104 n. 4, 118
epistemology, 3, 18, 36, 41, 108
Europe, 11, 119
Evans-Pritchard, E. E., 35
exchange of women, 12, 43 n. 2, 78, 92 n. 8, 117
exogamy, 1, 11, 12, 17, 19, 43 n. 1, 70, n. 5, 77, 94, 114, 117
explanatory strategy, 13, 16, 35, 42, 46–7, 62, 64

factions, 46, 81
Ferdinand, K., 92 n. 10
Fernea, R. A., 4, 8, 9
Fischer, M. M. J., 43 n. 5
Fodor, J. A., 115
Fortes, M., 118
Frazer, J., 105–6
frequency of FBD marriage, 4, 16, 22, 28, 31–2, 44 n. 10, 65–6, 70 n. 4, 81, 94, 103, 104 n. 5
Fuller, A. H., 33, 128 n. 11
function, 1–4, 35–9, 47–8, 56, 66, 68–9, 72, 79, 86, 90, 105, 110–14
functionalism, 36, 106

Galilee, 95, 101
Geertz, H., 1, 14 n. 2, 41, 43 n. 3, 66, 70 n. 5, 103 n. 1, 104 n. 1, n. 2
Gellner, E., 104 n. 6, 105, 107–9
gender relations, 2, 12, 119–20, 126–7
genealogy, 4, 44 n. 8, 46, 85, 87–9, 98, 100, 110, 118
Gilbert, J. P., 18, 34
Ginat, J., 122, 128 n. 11
Gluckman, M., 118
goals, 2, 63, 67, 69, 75–6, 85, 108

Index

Goldberg, H, M. 18, 34, 120
Good, A., 4, 43 n. 2
Goody, J., 4, 11, 12, 36, 43 n. 1, 62, 64, 112, 113, 119
Granqvist, H., 14 n. 2, 17, 43 n. 4, n. 5, 62, 124
Guichard, P., 70 n. 3
Gulick, J., 8

hadith, 119, 120
Hamawand, 32
Hammel, E. A., 18, 34
hamula, 80–5, 95–6, 98, 104 n. 1
Heath, A., 45
Hilal, J. M., 9, 32, 70 n. 3, 78, 120
Hobart, M., 107–9
Holy, L., 8, 14 n. 7, 36, 43 n. 5, 91 n. 2
Homans, G., 45
homogamy, 112
honour, 12, 72, 74–5, 119–26, 127 n. 5
Hopkins, K., 11
hypergamy, 70 n. 5, 112–14, 122, 124, 126, 127 n. 2
hypogamy, 70 n. 5, 112–13

ideology, 2, 4, 41, 46, 68, 77, 79, 81–2, 84–5, 87–90, 95, 98, 103, 104 n. 1, 111, 113, 117
incest, 28, 29, 33
inheritance, 12, 62–4, 70 n. 4, n. 5, 113–14, 119, 127 n. 1
inter-generational marriages, 25, 56–7
Iran, 14 n. 6, 34, 43 n. 6
Irons, W., 43 n. 5, 44 n. 8, 118, 123, 124, 128 n. 11
Islam, 119–22, 127 n. 3
Israel, 20, 21, 32, 80–1, 83, 86, 95, 98, 103 n. 1, 118, 122, 124

Jews, 32
Jordan, 95, 118

Kababish, 96–100
Kabyles, 26, 70 n. 7
Kangra, 101
Kaplan, J. O., 46
Kasdan, L., 5, 17, 22, 34, 46, 62, 70 n. 5, 85, 118
Keesing, R. M., 3, 105, 109
Keyser, J. M. B., 18, 43 n. 5
Khuri, F. I., 9, 43 n. 5, 63, 64, 67, 70 n. 3, 78, 113, 114, 127 n. 3, 128 n. 10, n. 11
kinship terminology, 19–20, 23–4, 26, 28–30, 44, n. 9, 56–7, 81, 85–7, 91 n. 5, 98, 104 n. 1
Komachi, 34
Koran, 23, 62–4, 70 n. 4, 113–14, 119, 127 n. 1
Kressel, G., 9, 77, 92 n. 9, 93, 104 n. 6, 124, 128 n. 11
Kufr al-Ma, 20, 95
Kunar, 94, 124
Kurdistan, 77
Kurds, 32

Lancaster, W., 14 n. 2, 15, 25, 33, 77, 88–90, 124, 127 n. 4
Larson, B. K., 41
Leach, E. R., 47
Lebanon, 20, 33, 95, 128 n. 11
Leech, G., 42
legitimisation, 64–5, 90, 93, 103
Levant, 12
Lévi-Strauss, C., 14 n. 3, n. 4, 19, 43 n. 2, 78
Lewis, I. M., 120, 128 n. 10
Lindholm, C., 126
lineage endogamy, 16–23, 26–7, 31, 34, 40–2
lineage model, 103 n. 1, 104 n. 1
linguistic model, 36
local endogamy, 16, 64
Lutfiyya, A. M., 43 n. 3, n. 4
Luzbetak, L., 11
Lyons, J., 42

McCabe, J., 43 n. 5
Maghreb, 20, 33, 92 n. 8
Magnarella, P. J., 120, 122, 127 n. 8
Maher, V., 19, 41, 66, 85
Malarkey, J. M., 4, 8, 9
marriage choices, 7–11, 30, 47, 61, 64–5, 67, 77, 89, 92 n. 10, 96
marriage negotiations, 48, 57–61, 67,

70 n. 2, 74
marriage pattern, 6–9, 11, 16–18,
    45–8, 64, 66–8, 77, 80, 95, 100, 103,
    117
marriage payments, 36–7, 122; *see also*
    bridewealth
marriage system, 10–12, 43 n. 2
Marri Baluch 26–32, 34, 125–6
Marx, E., 16, 43 n. 3, 44 n. 10, 86–7, 122,
    124, 128 n. 10
mathematical model, 18, 34
mechanical model, 14 n. 3, 17
Mediterranean, 11, 119
Meeker, M. E., 39, 67, 104 n. 2, 120–2,
    127 n. 7, 128 n. 8
Melanesia, 4
Mernissi, F., 119, 120
Milton, K., 39
Morocco, 14 n. 1, 43 n. 7, 70 n. 5,
    103 n. 1, 123
Murphy, R. F., 5, 17, 22, 34, 46, 62,
    70 n. 5, 85, 118
Musil, A., 14 n. 2, 124, 128 n. 10

Nassehi-Behnam, V., 43 n. 4
Needham, R., 5, 9
Negev, 34, 86–7, 90, 122, 123
norms, 6–7, 19, 54, 61–3, 70, 74–6, 78,
    83, 88, 91 n. 4, 98, 114, 116, 127 n. 2
North Africa, 13 n. 1, 119

Olesen, A., 122, 127 n. 7
Ortner, S. B., 35, 40, 47, 69

Pakhtun, 94, 124
Pakistan, 9, 14 n. 1, 34, 70 n. 2, 95
Parkin, D., 36, 39
Parry, J. P., 101, 127 n. 2
Pastner, C. Mc., 15, 43 n. 5, 66, 70 n. 2,
    85, 95, 104 n. 2, 121, 127 n. 4
Pastner, S., 15, 127 n. 4
Patai, R., 14 n. 2, 16–17, 20, 43 n. 4, 77,
    118
patronage, 12, 103 n. 1
patronymic association, 103 n. 1,
    104 n. 1
patronymic group, 80, 82, 103 n. 1, 112

Pehrson, R. N., 26–9, 85, 125
Peristiany, J. G., 127 n. 6
Peters, E. L., 11, 14 n. 2, 16–17, 25, 33,
    41, 43 n. 4, 62, 80, 85, 95, 103 n. 1,
    104 n. 2, n. 5, 123, 127 n. 5
Pierce, J. E., 14 n. 1, 127 n. 5
Pitt-Rivers, J., 6, 11, 12, 17, 43 n. 1, 78,
    104 n. 2, 121, 127 n. 6, n. 8
Pocock, D. F., 36
power, 93–7, 99, 101–3, 126
pragmatic reasons, 46, 61–4, 66–7, 110
prescription, 14 n. 4
property alienation, 62–4, 70 n. 5,
    112–14, 116–17
psychological motivation, 2

Randolph, R., 25, 34, 35, 43 n. 5, 44 n. 8,
    104 n. 6
Rassam, A., 104 n. 1, 120
residence after marriage, 55
Rivière, P. G., 5
Robertson Smith, W., 16, 17, 19, 124,
    127 n. 1
Rosen, L., 41, 67
Rosenfeld, H., 21–2, 62, 78, 95, 104 n. 2,
    n. 3, n. 6, 120, 128 n. 11
rules, 6, 8, 9, 14 n. 5, 47, 74–5
Rwala, 32–3, 77, 80, 88–90, 124

Sahlins, M., 68
Salim, S. M., 14 n. 2, 43 n. 3, 128 n. 11
Sampson, G., 115
Schapera, I., 78
Scheffler, H. W., 104 n. 1
Schneider, D. M., 45, 76
Schneider, J., 90, 122, 123, 127 n. 5
semantics, 36, 41, 115
sex, 12, 119–21
Shahsevan, 43 n. 6, 91 n. 7, 104 n. 7, 117
Skorupski, J., 38, 42, 43, 115
solidarity, 75–6, 82, 84, 90, 94, 98, 103,
    114, 117–18, 121–2; *see also* agnatic
    solidarity
Sperber, D., 61
statistical model, 14 n. 3
statistics, 6, 7, 10, 18, 21, 71 n. 6, 117
Stirling, P., 15, 43 n. 3, 121, 122, 127 n. 4,

n. 7
Stowasser, B. F., 119, 120
Strathern, M., 105, 106, 107
structural consequences, 1, 23, 45–6, 118
Stuchlik, M., 8, 36, 63
Sudan, 13, 14 n. 1, n. 7, 19, 95
Swat Pukhtun, 126
symbolic capital, 93–4, 100–2, 113
symbolic system, 13, 37, 47, 106

Tambiah, S. J., 64
Tapper, N., 10, 14 n. 6, 34, 121, 122, 123, 127 n. 5, n. 7
Tapper, R., 14 n. 6, 15, 34, 43 n. 3, n. 4, n. 5, n. 6, 91 n. 7, 92 n. 7, 93, 104, n. 7, 117, 120–3, 127 n. 4, n. 5. n. 7, 128 n. 8
Tillion, G., 11, 12, 20, 33, 43 n. 7, 62, 92, n. 8, 104, n. 2, 111, 113, 114
Tswana, 78
Tunisia, 118, 124

Turkey, 14 n. 1, 87, 91 n. 3, 123
Tyler, S., 108

Uberoi, J. P. S., 19

Van Sommers, P., 127 n. 5
Verdon, M., 4

Webster, S. K., 43 n. 7, 123
Wellhausen, J., 16, 17
Westermarck, E., 112
Whitehead, H., 35, 40, 47, 69
Wikan, U., 15, 127 n. 4

Yomut, 122
Yörük, 20, 43 n. 8, 123
Youssef, N. H., 66

Zikri Baluch, 70 n. 2, 95
Zoroastrianism, 14 n. 6, 34